CONSCIOUS LEADERSHIP IN ACTION!

FLOYD CARLSON

Conscious Leadership In Action!

First published in 2015 by

Panoma Press Ltd.
48 St Vincent Drive, St Albans, Herts, AL1 5SJ, UK
info@panomapress.com
www.panomapress.com

Book layout by Neil Coe.
Graphics created by Kelly Hanz from hanzondesign.

Printed on acid-free paper from managed forests.

ISBN 978-1-909623-92-7

The right of Floyd Carlson to be identified as the author of this work has been asserted in accordance with sections 77 and 78 of the Copyright Designs and Patents Act 1988.

A CIP catalogue record for this book is available from the British Library.

Dedication

To my amazing family – Ellen, Eric and Garrett.
Thank you for being with me on my journey!

Testimonials

"Floyd combines neuroscience, military leadership training and the corporate world, Eastern and Western traditions – all to serve an aspiring leader on the way to fulfillment."

Elena Khomenko
Leadership Development Consultant and Executive Coach

"Conscious Leadership in Action unveils the mysticism of transformational leadership. Impactful, practical and compelling, all leaders will benefit from the tools, exercises and lessons in this book. Leaders can easily incorporate them in a disciplined way and transform themselves, their teams, and organizations."

Tracy Cocivera, Ph.D.,
C.Psych Business Psychologist

"Floyd does an excellent job of providing countless exercises, examples and frameworks for leaders who are serious about raising their levels of leadership consciousness."

Suzanne Qualia,
MBA CIRM, Executive Leadership Coach

"If personal growth is a passion, this book is a must read! Conscious Leadership shook me awake to realize my impact in the world. Floyd brings the learning alive with tools in each section that helped me put the ideas into practice immediately."

Jennifer Dulin,
Director of Client Services, Blessing White

Table of Contents

Introduction

It is time to get out of the Stone Age of leading and embrace the choice to be conscious in how we live our lives and interact with each other. By reading this book you are stepping into your own journey of conscious leading and transforming your life. Congratulations for being courageous to want to make a positive change in who you are being and how you are showing up in life each day. Let's begin by understanding why conscious leading is so important.

Iraq, Operation Desert Storm – rumors persisted in our camp just inside the border of Saudi Arabia before the beginning of the ground offensive that the company commander was being targeted as a "frag candidate," meaning one of his own soldiers whom he was responsible for leading would arrange a fatal accident to happen to him. I was a first lieutenant and I was the unit's executive officer. From this position of being second in command, I witnessed first-hand the numerous friendly casualties one leader would inflict on the people he was entrusted to lead. These were not the wounds you could physically see, these were wounds that would last forever in their subconscious and continue to haunt them for years. The commander was a brilliant tactician who was the poster child of a theory X leader, meaning he over-relied on threats and coercion to gain his people's compliance. The atmosphere in the unit was punitive and full of mistrust. If you ended up on his list you would receive his wrath double. In our commander's mind, one of our lieutenants could not do anything right and was being constantly yelled at and singled out daily. The stress of pending combat was already extremely high, and this added pressure put the lieutenant in such a bad state that after being berated over the radio on our night move to our forward deployment position before we would enter Iraq, he cracked and could not take it anymore. The look on his face told the story; he had death in his eyes. I have seen this look before when I was younger and witnessed the look in a person's eyes before they committed a murder. I knew in my heart what would happen next unless action was taken. The lieutenant walked into the empty desert and I handed my weapon to my driver Castro and told him I was going out there to disarm the lieutenant. I also gave Castro my "in case I die" letter to my wife. I had no idea what would happen to me, but I knew if I did not intervene someone was going to die that night.

As I came closer to the lieutenant I showed him I was not carrying a weapon and just started talking with him. I focused on what was the most important thing in his life and who did he love the most. It was his family who was waiting for him back at home. We talked for about an hour and I could see his anger melt away. To be safe, and to allow him more time to cool down, I asked him for his firearm. He gave me his weapon and we walked together back to his vehicle. That night he was transferred to a unit in our battalion supply train. In the end, two of our three platoon leaders would be removed before we started the ground war. Our first sergeant was removed right after the ground war was completed. The stress of the situation and working for such a leader was unbearable. This may be an extreme example of what does not constitute a conscious leader, yet this true story illustrates that a leader can have a profound impact. A leader can inspire people, be unmemorable, or negatively impact their lives like the story above.

It has become all too common in corporations, especially since the financial crisis in 2008, to lead from a platform of fear. In a discussion about the possible results about an upcoming annual employee satisfaction survey, I saw a clear example of the fear mentality in action. To set the stage since 2008, the high-tech company where I was working had seen yearly double-digit budget cuts. Additionally, for five straight years there had been a minimum budget available to allow the employees the opportunity to develop their skills by taking training courses. In a discussion with a senior vice president of the firm, I highlighted what I believed would be the main area for possible negative feedback. To my surprise the senior leader highlighted the number of people who would have to be fired to allow people to take training; people should be grateful they have a job and it is very difficult out there in the job market. His full focus was that the employees should be scared and just be happy they have a job. The greater challenge is the daily impact of this leader: his perspective has an effect on the people reporting to him, and this becomes a cycle continuing throughout the entire organization. The impact to the organization and the people within it is huge. Fear is ramped; people are unhappy and not engaged. This situation highlights that the beliefs, fears and perceptions of a leader have a major impact on those they lead and how they themselves perform.

Are these stories unique or common? The news, research and personal stories people tell indicate these are not isolated incidents. In his article "Army Takes on its Own Toxic Leaders" (www.npr.org) dated January 6,

2014, Daniel Zwerdling highlights how the U.S. army publicly states they have a problem with too many "toxic leaders." These are leaders who make the lives of the people under their command miserable. In the article, research conducted by Dave Matsuda in 2010 of around 30 soldiers who committed or attempted suicide within one year in Iraq, found friends of these soldiers who remarked the leader's actions contributed to pushing the soldiers to this state. Further, the article highlights an additional study of more than 22,000 service members between 2009 and 2010, by the Center for Army Leadership at Fort Leavenworth, found that 20% of the respondents stated their leaders were what was defined by the study as toxic. The U.S. army's 2012 version of their leadership manual, Army Doctrine Publication 6–22, calls out toxic leadership and impact on the organization under the charter and ethics of leading by stating, "Leaders seen as abusive or toxic (such as intimidating and insulting subordinates) have higher rates of non-combatant mistreatment and misconduct in their units." Under setting the conditions for a positive climate the manual highlights, "Many view leadership by default as only positive actions. However, some leaders use inappropriate strategies to obtain immediate results and mindless adherence to orders without concern for others. They may bully others, berate subordinates mercilessly, or make unlawful choices to get their way. Selfish leaders ignore ideas from others, micromanage events, hoard information, undermine peers, and work to look good to superiors. Extreme and consistent forms of these undesirable behaviors indicate a toxic or abusive leader. Leaders with a positive approach can be firm in exacting discipline and can do so with care and respect for those they lead and in the interest of the organization's future." The good news for the army is defining and speaking about it is a first step to bringing more awareness of the situation. As we will discuss throughout this book, awareness is an essential step to creating change. With awareness different choices can occur and this leads to different results.

While toxic leaders can be the extreme, there are many other leaders who just do not have any real impact on their people at all. When I ask many people what percentage of the leaders they have worked with that they thought were good and they would want to work for again, I get below 27%. When I ask how many they would trust with their life, the numbers are a lot smaller. In his March 22, 2013 blog post titled "Beware of Managers From Hell," Gallup Chairman and CEO Jim Clifton highlights that of the roughly 100 million people in America who have full-time jobs, only 30%

feel they are engaged and inspired at work. He continues with 50% are not engaged and 20% are actively disengaged. In my own 30-year professional career with half being in the U.S. military and half being in a corporation, I can count only four. Three of them were in the military and only one was outside the military. These four leaders were very special and lived the traits that represent conscious leading to me. What made the difference of these leaders that I would want to work for again and distinguished them from all the others who didn't make an impact? These leaders had the following traits:

- They led by being an example. They did what they said they would and were consistent with their actions.

- They had high integrity and did what was right regardless of the situation, even if it made them look bad or would be the harder route to follow.

- They demonstrated empathy and knew their people. They gave the feedback you rarely receive that truly moves you to be better.

- They cared more for their people than themselves.

- They checked their ego at the door daily and led from their heart.

- They were loyal to their people and were trusting.

- They made a positive difference for their people, team, company, community and everyone they met.

- They were being in spirit, connected to their source of energy, being a higher consciousness.

- They knew how to manage their energy daily and show up in the right mood for the situation.

- They were continuously working on themselves to be better.

These traits are foundational elements to conscious leading. Conscious leading is taking consistent actions that make a positive difference for your people, family, friends, community, organizations, and environment, while making the world a better place to live. A conscious leader is everyone who makes the decision to be one, believes in their heart they are a leader and takes the steps to live and be an example for the world to follow. Being a conscious leader is an ongoing journey and the personal wisdom that you gain, learn and apply along the way.

The reason I have written this book is to provide you with a guide to help you along your way of developing yourself in conscious leading. Experiencing the type of leadership that my commander in Desert Storm lived by, and seeing so many poor examples of people leading, has inspired me to want to lead from a new paradigm of making a positive difference. This guide is a product of the things I have tried and learned along my journey so far to be the best I can be at conscious leading. Being on this trip has been a constant learning environment and I'm still learning every day. To help you with gaining a deeper experience I have included a number of exercises and tools you can use. The best way to learn is by doing the exercises as you go through the material. I find life is like a marathon and it is your race to run. You are running against yourself, just like each of us is doing in our life daily, we are facing challenges and working to overcome them. In this life race you are looking to find your own pace. As a coach I can help you with your training, nutrition and lessons learned from my races and experience; I can also help you to be more efficient and effective while doing it and this will help you. In the end though, I cannot run the race for you. Only you can, so find what works for you and incorporate it in your daily life.

To help you run your race I have divided the book into two parts. Part I: Transforming Yourself To Have The Life Of Your Dreams covers those subjects to assist you with your personal change to being a conscious leader in your daily life. Chapter 1 begins with the essential element you need to fuel your transformation; your peak energy. Your energy you have every day and how you show up to the world either supports your personal success or drains it to give you more of what you have today. By applying the techniques and tools covered within this section, you will start to gain the energy you need for making the changes you want to have in your life. Chapter 2 helps you to identify what is holding you back from achieving the success you deserve in your life. Chapters 3 and 4 give you many tools and rituals to implement to run your life race at your pace and build within you the precious gift of being happy. Happiness is within all of us to claim; live it and sustain it with your daily success rituals that work just right for you.

Part II: Being A Leader Of Your Transformation And Making A Difference For Others dives deeper into your leadership, what it means to be a leader and how you can build a plan to implement conscious leadership into your entire organization. In Chapter 5, we discuss together that everyone is a leader. You do not need a business card saying you are a leader to be one. Leadership comes in many forms and in many situations, all you need to do is make the choice to be a leader in everything you do and be the great example for others to follow. Chapter 6 gives insights into where conscious leading can take us as individuals, a society, a business and where your creativity can lead to a better future for everyone. In the spirit of making this an action manual, Chapter 7 gives more tools and techniques you can apply and implement to create your leadership transformation. Finally in Chapter 8 we cover organizational transformation. When people who are on a similar journey get together each person's personal energy expands. Bring an entire group of people together with their expanded personal energy and you are creating something magical. You will have a conscious organization that will benefit every stakeholder.

To be one of those unforgettable leaders, to inspire others with your wonderful example, to find what makes you most happy and just do more of it, to discover new tools and techniques, to bring more awareness and consciousness into your life, it is time to begin your personal journey to create your own transformation, as it will unfold for you. I acknowledge your courage to run your life race and be the best you can be by taking action by reading this book and doing the work to change your life. Your legend is yet to be written so enjoy the journey of **Conscious Leadership In Action!**

PART I

Transforming Yourself To Have The Life Of Your Dreams

CHAPTER 1

Peak Energy: Your State For Transformed Leadership

Managing your peak energy is the juice to drive change in your life

Imagine every day waking up and having the life of your dreams and your destiny come true. Your day is like a well-executed play, where the movements and timings are choreographed to perfection. You feel amazing, alive, and full of energy. Everything you do is effortless and feels natural. Your connections with your customers, peers, friends and family are enriched, as your conversations are deep, gratifying and meaningful. You do not want this day to ever end and when you finally are ready to fall asleep you have an amazing sense of peace and accomplishment playing through your mind. Your last thought is well done, fantastic day, I can't wait to do it again even better tomorrow!

You are probably saying to yourself this is fantasy and what is this guy smoking? My position is this is not just an imaginary dream that is not achievable. This is a reality that everyone can achieve in their life. The journey will take effort, discipline, willpower and action on your part to make it happen. This is not like leaving the Shire and facing the perils of Middle Earth to throw the ring into the fires of Mordor. You may have a belief or two similar to this today, which has interfered with you having the life of your dreams every day. This is all about you and taking actions that will help you to achieve more happiness and find your true self. This book is your guide to lead you on your personal and organizational transformation.

Before we can begin your journey I want to clarify the meaning of "find your true self." Finding your true self is going within yourself and realizing the answer to your happiness is and has always been inside you. It is stripping away the self-defeating beliefs, self-judgment, not listening to your inner critic voice, non-supporting habits and being caught up in the need for external events, people and situations to make you happy. There is nothing wrong with wanting or having a bigger house, more money, new vehicle, taking trips or important job title. This guide will even help you with those goals. However, when these are your primary focus and what you constantly seek, believing this will give you everlasting happiness, and when you get them you still feel you are missing something out of life, it is finding your true self that will fill this emptiness. I have learned this through what I call the illusion of command. When I was an enlisted soldier I saw my lieutenant and said to myself I can do this. The only real difference between him and me is around three years of college. When I'm a lieutenant I will have all this opportunity to lead and make changes. When I did become a second lieutenant my thoughts went to just wait until I am a first lieutenant. This continued for captain and then major. Each time I was seeking more even while the new rank was being pinned on. I had this same realization when I was seeking my goal to get promoted to director. I knew achieving this goal was a major milestone to move me higher up the corporate ladder. In my mind title equals great success. When the promotion came, yes that particular moment brought me brief happiness, yet I was already moving my sights to now I can go after being a senior director and gave myself a three-year time frame to achieve it. I took no time to either really enjoy the moment or appreciate the accomplishment. I was seeking bigger and greater responsibility and influence, I would say to myself just wait till I'm a senior director, I'll be even happier. This has been a theme throughout my life and when I became aware of it, I was then able to change it. Awareness is an essential tool for your transformation, which I will cover in more depth throughout the book.

Am I alone in this feeling? When I spoke to a vice president who had recently attended a meeting in their company of 50 top leaders, a key discussion was around how they each felt they did not have enough budget, people or resources to be successful. A guest former CEO speaker stopped the group and asked how many of the company's people reported to the 50 leaders in the room. The answer was nearly 35,000 employees and this was still not enough. The speaker's wisdom at that moment was to highlight that the people work for you and not the CEO. When he was a CEO his direct reports told him the same thing. He told the group it was up to them to make a difference for the people they have in their care and focus on them. The former CEO brought awareness to the group to see beyond the daily script they have running in their head that they need more to be successful and more success will bring happiness. In reality, more brings the belief you need to have even more to be truly happy and this becomes the seeking game for more, bigger and greater that traps many of us. The good news is we can change this by focusing on our personal transformation.

The biggest asset you have to fuel your personal transformation is how you manage your energy, what you focus on and how you spend your time. The interconnected model below highlights how your energy management and focus have an impact on your overall confidence, courage and taking bold action, plus unlocking your full potential. The three components:

- Energy management and focus.

- Building your confidence, courage and being bold.

- Unlocking your full potential by being in your peak energy state.

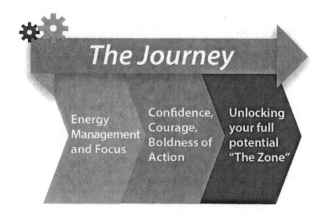

Building and strengthening any one of these three components expands and causes growth in the other areas. For example, as you do something to increase your energy and this helps you to do something you have not completed before, such as finish a 10-kilometer race in less than 45 minutes. This builds your confidence in your running, which helps you to unlock your running potential of a new personal best or prepare you for the next level of running distance like a half-marathon.

Energy management and focus is being aware of what gives you energy, what drains your energy, and managing your energy levels throughout the day. Focus is being aware of your thoughts and where you place your attention. Think of this as those activities and things that give you the most juice in your life. These elements are the tools that will drive your change. They will help you to be more positive and as you focus on this you will attract more of the positive things you want in your life.

Building your confidence, courage and being bold is feeling you cannot fail; you face your fears and do it anyway. You are willing to do those things you have felt are too hard and you could never do them. While facing these challenges you take bold action and take another step forward in your transformation. A secret I have found is the more I become aware of my lifelong habits that have been holding me back and start to let them go, confidence and courage shows up for me with little effort. These help me to want to do even more work to let go of even more things holding me back.

Unlocking your full potential is being in your zone of peak energy, where everything is going incredibly well. You are enjoying the moment; you are lost in time, happy and feeling fantastic. I find when I am fully connected to others and they are to me, being in this zone becomes so easy. I am able to create even more and greater things with others than if I do it alone.

The personal implications when these elements are all aligned and fueling each other is you have a feeling of wellbeing, you are in your zone. When you watch a sports team or athlete performing at their very best, it looks effortless, they are making all the right passes, making all the right moves, their body, energy and feeling are acting as one. This is being in the zone, when your energy, focus, confidence reaches a crescendo and you are being your best in that moment. Achieving this starts with how you manage your energy. From the time you wake to the time you go to bed, how effectively you perform energy management will determine how successful you are in achieving the life of your dreams.

To demonstrate the connection of these three elements, I have always been an avid runner in my life. I find running is an activity that gives me energy, and I now use this activity six times a week, because of how this makes me feel and provides the juice to fuel my life. After moving to Brussels I ran my first Brussels 20K race on May 27, 2001. This was a big step up in distance for me as normally I would run for 30–45 minutes, every other day. I did not focus or schedule the time to train properly for the event. On the day of the race it was a warm day of around 28 degrees Celsius, and I did not take in the right nutrients or fluids to give me the energy I needed for the distance. I did feel confident that I could finish the race and had visions of completing the race in a decent time. When the cannon went off in Jubilee Park to start the race, my confidence started to drop as the kilometers began to increase. I had thought Brussels was more flat, but the route was a continuous up and down. I did finish the race with a time of approximately one hour and 56 minutes (they did not use time chips back then to measure your time accurately). I felt ill and was wiped out by the effort. I had no energy to do anything else that day, except to go home and lie down for the next three hours. That evening I was able to reflect on what had gone wrong and captured the lessons in my running journal that I learned. There were many things I learned and the essential point for this discussion is I did not have the optimal energy, focus or preparation to be in my peak energy state for the race. This had the knock-on effect of impacting my confidence during the event when I needed it most and I never achieved my full potential that day. Applying these lessons has transformed my running and other aspects of my life. For example, on Sunday August 27, 2005 I ran the Brussels Half Marathon in 1:34:28, had the energy to compete in a golf tournament and go out for the evening with family and friends for dinner. It all started with managing my energy to its peak level.

How to maximize your energy

To maximize your energy, understanding the sources that give you energy is important. Sources are anything that enables you and affects your energy. In this section you will see how these different components interact and you will take action to determine your energy sources.

In the diagram below there are six areas that impact the amount of energy you will have daily to achieve the life of your dreams. If any one of these areas is draining you and not energizing you, your ability to be at peak energy will be off. You will also see there is an enabler that can either multiply the energy you have in each area or non-energy as this also can become an energy drainer.

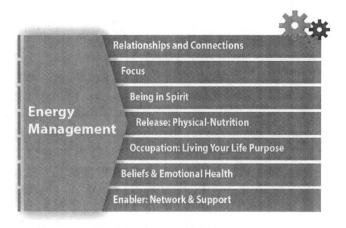

Relationships and Connections:

How does your relationship with your loved ones, family, friends, colleagues, team members and others impact your energy? Do they energize or not? Are there specific relationships that work for you and ones that do not? It is time to assess your relationships. The intent is to give you awareness of the people and specific things about your relationships that are giving you energy or are draining you. In this exercise you will assess your relationships.

1. List each of your closest relationships on a piece of paper, spreadsheet or in your journal.

2. Next to each relationship put a zero to five to rate the level of energy this relationship provides you. Zero is low, meaning the relationship truly drains your energy and you feel spent and tired after interacting with this person. Five means you feel energized and great being with this person. One through four is your gage of how you feel between the definitions of zero and five. For this exercise use the average of your overall interaction with the person.

3. Once you have gone through and rated the relationship to energy feeling, look at each person and jot down to the right of the score brief bullets that highlight how you would characterize what energizes you in this relationship and what actually drains you. See figure below.

Jenifer	5	Listens to me without judgment; is always there for me; Makes me laugh
Tom	2	Always correcting me; thinks he knows it all
Pam	4	Solid friend who cares; fun to be with
Tina	0	Talks about me and others behind our backs; she makes me feel horrible about myself with her constant criticism

4. Now analyze the items you have listed next to the different relationships that you have and determine are there any common themes appearing, for both energizers and drainers.
5. Somewhere on your paper list the top five things about your relationships that energize you and top five drainers.

Focus:

Where you place your attention and focus is where your energy is diverted to. This is very powerful for transforming your life by placing your focus on those things you want to achieve and things that energize you. This is because your mind will support you and help you with what you are focusing on. We filter information that we take in based on where we are placing our focus. For example, if you and I go to your local Mini car dealership to look at their new models, the minute we leave the parking lot we will start seeing Minis everywhere. We did not see them before, but now our focus is on the Mini we see them everywhere. This is the same for many factors in our life. If you are let go from your company and your focus is there are no opportunities in this economy, you will get exactly that, no opportunities because that is where your focus is. Another example: if before you go into a key meeting or presentation and ask yourself "am I ready?" your mind will look for any and every time you were not prepared and show you all these examples. This gets into power questions, which we will cover later to help you in these situations. These examples demonstrate the power of focus.

Where do you place your focus today? In your journal or on a piece of paper answer the following questions:

1. What are you focusing on? Are they things that make you feel energized or things that just consume calories and do not make you feel you are at your best? Do you spend your time worrying about the future, or what someone may say or has said that makes you angry? List examples of where you place your focus.

2. What would you rather be focusing your attention toward? List those things you would rather be doing instead of the items from question one.

3. What is preventing you from focusing on the things you just listed?

4. What actions can you take now to start focusing on the things you want?

Being in Spirit:

Being in spirit is what you are doing that connects you with your inner self, your higher spirit or consciousness, God or any other activity that gives you a sense of connection with something bigger than your daily life. This can come from spending time in nature, praying, meditation, yoga or any of many things that give you an inner peaceful feeling. If you are feeling you are missing something in your life, this may be a source of personal energy to consider. I had neglected this energy source for years and when I realized it, I took the action to start focusing on my spirituality. I did this by reading books such as *The Power of Now* by Eckhart Tolle, *The Monk Who Sold his Ferrari* by Robin Sharma, *The Big Leap* by Gay Hendricks and others. I also started with yoga and meditation. I found Kundalini yoga gave me a great start in my meditation practice and helped me to feel more relaxed and I felt I had more energy.

In your journal or on a piece of paper answer the following questions:

1. When you look at being in spirit, on a rating of zero to five (zero low, five high), how would you rate this area today in your life in relation to how much does this give you energy?

2. How important is it for you to focus on this energy source in your life?

3. What activities would you like to start doing to help develop this energy source to raise your rating from question one?

4. Who can help you with developing this area?

5. What actions can you start to take today and schedule in your calendar?

Release – Physical – Nutrition:

The quickest way to change your energy is through increasing your physical activity and changing your diet. Doing sport will help you to release tension and stress and brings more focus and clarity. In my life, running and biking in the morning six times a week gives me the energy I need for the entire day. I feel more relaxed and calm throughout my day. It does not take a lot to get started. Find the physical activity that works best for you. This can be walking, riding, swimming, running, canoeing or whatever.

I have seen amazing changes in people's lives by just making changes in this energy source. In the company I worked for in Brussels, we started a "start to run" program to offer fun activities and bring people together. I was asked to co-lead based on my passion for running and I was also one of the coaches. We selected a 5K race in Bruges, Belgium in 10 weeks as a capstone event for the new runners to have a target. We did a 10-week program that consisted of three training sessions a week. An example of a session for week 1 was a 20-minute session where it consisted of 10 minutes' walking and 10 minutes' running. Giorgio was one of the new runners and he had never done any real sport except what he had done in school as part of gym class, and he was overweight. I walked and ran with him on those sessions and he struggled to complete the exercise at his pace. I stayed with him and continued to encourage him to do what he could. Giorgio began to get in better condition and with it he started to lose weight and have energy he did not have before. The knock-on effect was this started to have a positive impact in all the other areas in his life. Since the "start to run" program, he has gone on to run marathons and has become an avid runner. The key is as he said, "Running has become for me a lifestyle, which I am enjoying very, very much in everything else I do." Physical activity gave him the energy he needed to give him a spark in all areas of his life.

The same goes for your diet, this includes what you eat and drink. Like with physical activity it is finding what works best for you. Become aware of how you feel after you eat certain foods or drink certain drinks. Does the meal give you energy or not? Drinking water to ensure you are hydrated can go a long way to giving you more energy. In his book *Spontaneous Happiness*, Dr. Andrew Weil highlights the value of a Mediterranean diet and how something as simple as caffeine can have dramatic impacts on your mood and happiness. I tried the experiment he suggests with decreasing my caffeine intake and sure enough I had a headache for two days once I stopped drinking coffee and after, I felt much better. I also have had more weight loss by changing my diet to eating more salad, leaner meats and reducing deep-fried products such as French fries, than from just doing sport. This has had a great impact on my feeling more energetic and helping me to run faster by losing more weight.

In your journal or on a piece of paper answer the following questions:

1. When you look at physical – nutrition, on a rating of zero to five (zero low, five high), how would you rate this area today in your life in relation to how much does this give you energy?

2. How important is it for you to focus on this energy source in your life?

3. What activities would you like to start doing to help develop this energy source to raise your rating from question one?

4. Who can help you with developing this area?

5. What actions can you start to take and schedule in your calendar?

6. What changes in your diet can you start to make and commit to?

Occupation – Living Your Life Purpose:

For many people this area consumes the greatest amount of their time and a huge amount of their energy. Does your occupation make you feel energized or does it drain you? I had the opportunity to take a vacation in South Africa where my partner and I were on a wine tour of the Western Cape region. As we were there in August, which is during their winter period, we had access to all of the wine makers at the different wineries we visited. It also helped that our guide personally knew them all. What amazed me was the incredible passion every one of them showed when they spoke about what they did and how they did it. This energized me just by being in their presence. When I'm talking about energy in what you do, this example is what I'm asking you about: does your job bring out all your passion and energy?

As we did with your relationship energy source, look at which parts of your occupation are working for you and which parts are not. It is time to assess your occupation. The intent is to give you awareness of the parts of your job that are giving you energy or are draining your energy. In this exercise you will assess your job.

1. On a piece of paper, spreadsheet or in your journal make two columns. Name one of the columns the "things about my job that energize me." Name the other column the "things about my job that drain my energy."

2. Take your time and under each column list those things you do daily, weekly, monthly or yearly that either give you energy or don't. If you enjoy an activity, get lost in time when you do it and feel great about it, this is an energizer.

3. Once you have completed two lists, look at each column and analyze the items you have listed. Are you seeing any common themes appearing, for both energizers and drainers?

4. What activities would you like to start doing more of to increase your energy in your job?

5. What activities would you like to stop doing to increase your energy in your job? Is there a way these can be swapped with someone who enjoys them? Can you make more fun (like making a game out of them or listen to music while doing them)?

6. What actions can you take to start increasing your energy from your job?

Beliefs and Emotional Health:

Your beliefs and where you emotionally spend your time will impact the energy you have. It takes a lot of your energy if you are spending your time in areas such as feeling unworthy, bitter, afraid, angry, bored, victimized, ashamed, hopeless etc. Your energy is low and you are sending out this low energy level to others. In turn they will respond to you based on what you are sending out. On the other hand, by feeling emotions of love, happiness, freedom, gratitude, compassion and passion you are in a high-energy state and this is where you will start to feel you are in the flow. Your relationships and interactions will be positively impacted by this high state of energy you are sending out. For example, when you are at a party or an event, who are the people you are naturally attracted to and you tend to gravitate to? It is normally the person giving out the most positive energy. Your emotional state impacts a number of the other energy sources we have already discussed and changes here have a major impact on the overall energy you will have.

Your emotional state is closely tied to your beliefs, thus I have put the two together. If you have the belief you are not worthy, you will also have this feeling and you will be transmitting this to others. I was fortunate to have a leader who gave me the type of feedback you rarely get. This is a key trait to being a conscious leader and having a conscious organization that I will cover in depth later. He summarized first by saying, "You and I were the same grade when you started working for me, and had timing been different, I could have been working for you." He continued with, "Now that I am a director and on track to senior director, I cannot figure out why you have not been promoted yet to director. You have all the skills, experience and talent. Matter of fact, I asked my coach about you and my coach came back with two questions. Does he really want it? And does he feel worthy?" Wow, this is the type of feedback that you will rarely get. I thought long and hard on these two questions and my answer to both was no. I now had the awareness and realization I had to do deeper work on myself. I had to challenge my belief on not being worthy, because this was also sending out a message to others. I did the work and by changing this belief the energy I was sending out changed and within a year I was promoted to director. The connection of belief to emotion is powerful. By making changes in your beliefs you will start to experience different outcomes for the better in your life.

Emotions and what we do to avoid and try to relive them can come in many forms. What I find and have experienced is when trying to relive a past event in the hopes of recreating the hit of the past emotion, it never has the exact same feeling. Yet many people try to recreate the exact experience over and over again. Being tied to these expectations almost always does not work. The lesson learned is to just be in the moment and accept it as it is and create a new experience with the feelings and emotions of this event.

In this exercise you will assess your beliefs and emotions you are living in to bring you awareness of what areas are consuming your energy.

1. On the list below, circle the emotions and beliefs that you are most feeling on a regular basis. Feel free to add any that are not listed.

Unworthiness	Bored	Freedom	Excited	Believing
Grief	Disappointed	Love	Acceptance	Cheerful
Anger	Resentful	Happiness	Appreciation	Motivated
Revenge	Hurt	Trust	Bliss	Revitalized
Worry	Misunderstood	Empowered	Courage	Cherished
Doubt	Frustrated	Passionate	Joy	Peaceful
Blame	Forgiveness	Positive	Enlighten	Energized
Sadness	Fear	Compassion	Optimism	Fortunate
Judgmental	Despair	Eager	Adored	Exhilarated
Bitter	Rage	Gratitude	Ambitious	Harmonious
Depression	Unhappy	Belief	Balanced	Dynamic
Hatred	Impatient	Confidence	Capable	Conscious

2. For each item you circled or added, rate them from a one to 10 (one low, 10 high) on how deep you believe and feel that emotion. For example, if you circled anger, how strong a factor is this in your life? If you feel anger regularly and it has a major impact then rate it a 10.

3. Now prioritize your list with the highest scoring items at the top. For example, if you had anger as a 10, unworthiness as a nine, worry as a nine, your list would be: 1) Anger – 10; 2) Unworthiness & Worry – 9.

4. Next to each item on your list, add brief bullets that highlight how you would characterize what causes you to feel that way or who causes you to feel that way. Do the best you can, there is no right or wrong answer and no judgment. It is just your view of what causes you to feel this emotion or have this belief.

5. Now analyze the items you have listed next to the different emotions and beliefs that you have highlighted and determine are there any common themes appearing. Are there any common triggers that

you recognize that cause the emotions to appear? These themes and triggers are your guides to focus on further to understand better what is causing the emotion and belief and begin taking steps to change it.

Network and Support:

Your network and support acts as an enabler to each of the energy management components. Do you have a mentor, coach, confidant, support group or specific people who bring the best creativity and energy out of you? These are people who can help you on your transformation and discuss the insights and awareness you have gained from the exercises above. These are people who are supportive and yet will challenge you to dig deeper and ask you questions to further your investigation. These are also people who have earned the opportunity to help you based on the trust you have developed together. You have each other's back and care about each other. It is time to assess your network. The intent is to give you awareness of whether you have anyone or any group that can help you increase your energy. In this exercise you will assess your support network.

·1. For each of the energy management components listed below write the name or group of a mentor, confidant or supportive friend who can help be part of your network

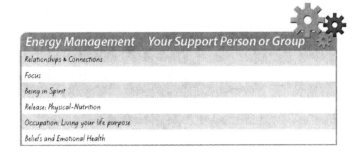

Energy Management	Your Support Person or Group
Relationships & Connections	
Focus	
Being in Spirit	
Release: Physical-Nutrition	
Occupation: Living your life purpose	
Beliefs and Emotional Health	

2. Who else do you know who does this area well in their life that could be part of your support network? Write their name next to the corresponding component.

3. Where else can you find a group or someone who can be part of your network?

4. Take action: reach out to the people or groups you have highlighted to start collaborating with them to be part of your network. Let them know what you have found in your analysis of your energy management system and how you admire that they do that area well and would like their help in understanding how they do it.

5. Have fun and enjoy it!

These six components and one enabler, along with the exercises you have just completed are your starting point to understand how the different components give or drain your energy. This awareness will help you to take action to expand your energy to be in your peak energy state.

How do you expand your energy to be in peak energy state?

Your daily goal is to be in a balanced state across the six energy management system components. I call this the zone of balance, where all six energy cells are roughly at the same level of energy as the other cells. In this state you have taken the actions to give you the energy to live the life of your dreams. From this balanced state of energy real magic begins when you connect and collaborate with others who are in their own balanced state of energy. From the diagram below this is when you are in the expansion of energy and are reaching your full potential. By supporting and building on each other, your energy expands greater than you can achieve by yourself. You feel you can achieve anything and your energy is working to support both of you. The diagram below highlights this interconnection.

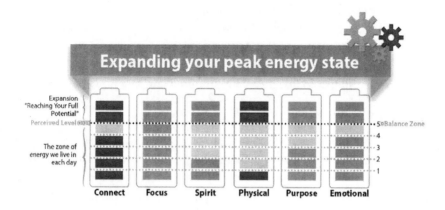

The picture might give you the impression that each cell is a standalone and by being great in one you will have the energy to sustain what you really want to achieve. The borders between the cells are transparent. One area can be so draining it will impact all the areas. You will be out of balance until you take the actions to eliminate and change the drainer to an energizer. Some people make the mistake of thinking the borders are hardened. They will focus all their attention on their career and neglect all the other areas. This may be a short-term strategy that works for you, but in the long run this will lead to burnout and overall unhappiness.

As you look at each of the energy sources and taking into account the exercise we have just completed to bring awareness to where you are with each energy component, you will see on the diagram a zero through five marking across each of the energy sources. For this exercise, put a solid line across each energy source that corresponds to the rating you feel most represents that area in your life today. For example, if you had rated being in spirit as a two, put a line across the two. Complete this for each of the six energy sources. You now have a view of what areas are your strengths that are going well to give you the energy you need to achieve your goals and dreams and those areas you need to work on. Your goal is first to reach your zone of balance, where each of the six components is working to support you. It only takes one area to impact all the others.

Activities to Expand your Energy

The above exercise is to give you a visual aid to guide your action plan to expand your energy. What are the activities that you can do to expand your energy? These exercises and tools are to help you do this and once you complete them, determine which things will work best for you and will become part of your action plan.

Exercise: Things that juice you!

In your journal or on a piece of paper list all the things that juice you, create passion, happiness and joy in your life. Answer these questions:

- How do these make you feel?

- Who are you being when you are doing these activities?

- How can you increase being and doing more of these activities each day?

- How can any of these be used to help give you more energy in any of the energy sources you want to grow your energy in?

- What can you schedule in your calendar right now that you are committed to start doing more of immediately?

Exercise: Past steps to success!

Your past is a great place to gain wisdom on what has worked well for you. Success will leave footprints and for this exercise you want to find these footprints. Answer these questions:

- While looking at your past, were there any times where you were excited and full of energy?

- What were you doing, who were you doing it with, how did this make you feel?

- How can you do or use this today to expand your energy?

Tool: Journaling for your success!

Journaling is a powerful tool to help you focus, and as we discussed under the focus energy component, where you focus is where you gain more awareness, and as with the mini example you start seeing more of it in your life. If you want to increase your gratitude, in your journal capture daily the top five things that day you are grateful for. If you want to increase your intuition, record those things that you felt intuitive on that day. If you want to increase your faith, write down in your success journal those things that gave you faith that day. This can be done for anything, such as what energized you that day, what top five successes did you have etc. The key is writing them down, it helps you to focus on them and get more of this in your life.

Tool: Managing your state!

How you show up with your energy is the number one impact to your mood and personal success. A great presentation is when the speaker has high energy, is physically engaged, confident, comfortable and enthusiastic. Walter Chrysler said, "The real secret of success is enthusiasm." Managing your state is showing up in your highest energy state. The quickest way to do it is to change your body position. This is using these actions to help you:

- Making eye contact that is engaging and warm.

- Being enthusiastic and genuinely excited to be there.

- Handshake and greeting. Confident and friendly.

- Smile – let the world see you smile.

- Posture – stand up and sit up straight.

- Matching state with your audience or person you are meeting with. If they speak fast, you need to match their pace.

Tool: Power questions!

Starting your day or when the situation is high state and the pressure is on most people tend to think negative questions. This has a major impact on your energy and state. In her recording on Heal Negative Charges, October 31, 2010, Ann Taylor (http://www.innerhealing.com) highlights that the average person has 60,000 thoughts a day and 77% of them are negative. That is a whopping 46,200 non-productive thoughts a person has each day. The kicker is 95% of the thoughts are the same thoughts they had the day before. These negative thoughts and emotions are destructive. To overcome this, change the questions you ask yourself and make them positive. For example, when you wake up in the morning you can ask yourself such questions as: who do I love, who loves me and how does that make me feel? What am I committed to? What is wonderful in my life? What am I excited about in my life? What am I really happy about in my life? What will I do today that makes a difference? For high stakes situations such as an important presentation you can ask yourself: how will I celebrate after this? What is the best way to inspire them? The goal is to use power questions to change your energy to support you.

⏀ Tool: Take a nap!

I find taking a 20–30-minute nap after my Sunday long runs for my marathon training is a great tool to increase my alertness and energy. If you find your energy is low, taking a nap can go a long way to boost your alertness, performance and energy.

These exercises and tools will help you with your overall transformation and build the energy you need to achieve it. It is essential you take action and schedule the things you have just gone through above. It is simple: the things that get scheduled will get done. It is easy to do nothing and if you want the life of your dreams then taking action is what will get you there. Pareto's 80/20-rule plays an important role when taking action. Twenty per cent of your actions will net 80% of your results, so to improve your success take more action and review which 20% are giving you the biggest returns. Once these things become clearer to you, do more of the things giving you the results and change the ones that are not giving you the results you desire.

Energy traps to avoid

The previous section helped you to identify which of the six energy management components you need to focus on and gave you some exercises and tools to help you expand your energy in those areas to improve your overall energy. When you reviewed the six energy components and conducted the exercises you also identified things that are draining your energy. In this section we look at energy traps that impact you reaching your peak energy state, your personal growth and success. The key again is to become aware of the traps and scripts you act out based on your environment and your inner voice/critic. These are tied to your beliefs, environmental conditioning throughout your life and your habits.

I will use an example from my life to demonstrate this and the impact on my mood at that time and overall energy. One Sunday I was in a great energy state that afternoon and my son was heading back to university but could not find the key to his bike he had left at the train station. Time was ticking and he was going to be late for the train and the next morning he had an exam he needed to take. This triggered my first belief that you are responsible for your own stuff and this started my energy to drain. As I helped him search everywhere within the house to locate his keys, he started to think the worst case scenario that he would just skip the test on Monday. This triggered and pushed my second button: don't give up. Now my script was starting to play in my head and I was getting mad, which further drained my energy. My son then went into victim mode and started to say how things like this always happen to him. From the tools we discussed in the last section, he was asking non-powering questions and his energy was greatly depleted and this triggered my third belief: you get what you focus on, so change your thoughts if they don't work. With all three of my buttons pushed based on my beliefs, my energy was pulled down and I was caught up in the drama.

What do you do when you find yourself in this situation like I did? Find out why your energy is being drained without judging yourself and be compassionate as you do it. A great way to start is asking yourself questions.

- What assumptions may I be making that may not be true?

- Am I taking this personally?

- Am I taking the situation too seriously?

- What about this situation is causing my energy to be drained?

- What beliefs do I have that are playing out with this situation?

- Is there any action I can take right now to make a positive difference in this situation?

Asking these questions and journaling on this event gave me the insight and awareness of which beliefs were in play and this helped me to look at how I could move from being in reaction mode to being in responding mode.

In another example of energy traps, Tim received a text message from his son saying, "Dad, the police came to the house asking for you." Tim's energy and state was changed instantly. He quickly called his son back and asked what they wanted. Tim's son said they wanted to know when Tim would be home. Tim then went into the mode of asking himself what this could be about. His mind was racing and his subconscious started to show every possibility, even to the worst-case example of what he could have possibly done wrong in the last five years. Tim was picturing all the possible things he could have done wrong. His body responded by sending him into fight, flight or freeze mode and a high level of stress. In this state Tim's body releases hormones that are meant to help him survive. The hormones are designed to help us run faster and fight harder. Once released they increase your heart rate and blood pressure, while delivering greater levels of oxygen and blood sugar to power important muscles. Our attention is completely focused on the threat and nothing else. This greatly improves our ability to survive from the pending danger. The challenge is this makes the person anxious, irritable, impacts their ability to work with others effectively, and with focusing on the threat intensely their judgment is impaired. Staying in this state continuously can impact your health. This event was using all of Tim's energy. Why was Tim in a mental script of worry about something when he did not even know what it was about? Is it Tim's association that if the police are asking for you by name it has to be something bad? How many times a day does something similar occur when someone says something, writes something or something is perceived that creates the same reaction in others and you? Tim was unable to sleep that night and continued to feel stressed the entire next day, until finally the following evening the police came to Tim's home and spoke to him. None of the worst-case scenarios he had perceived were related to the situation. It was someone claimed his car bumped theirs and the police were just completing the formality of the paperwork as there was no collaborating evidence the claim was true.

The issue for Tim is this is not an isolated reaction. Tim regularly creates stress response to events in his environment that occur at home, work or someone cutting him off on the road. Being in constant stress based on triggers in his environment is impacting Tim's ability to enjoy life and his overall happiness. At a minimum Tim's transformation opportunity is to take action to reduce the stress in his life. Examples include finding a release mechanism such as physical activity like walking, swimming, biking, running or another activity. It could be reading, listening to music, spending time in nature or whatever works best for you. A relaxation technique to reduce stress highlighted in *Words Can Change Your Brain* by Andrew Newberg and Mark Waldman is to breathe in for a count of five and exhale for a count of five doing both slowly. This is repeated three times and then you yawn a few times. By doing this you will feel more relaxed. The greater transformation change is for Tim to gain control over the triggers that are causing him to go into his stress routine. Tim can achieve this by using a number of techniques. For example, he could use a Neuro-Linguistic Programing (NLP) technique called the Swish Patterns. I learned this pattern from NLP Master Lynda Dyer from Sydney, Australia. Fundamentally this works by Tim getting a picture of the situation he wants to change. He would then create a picture of the behavior he wants to replace it with. Tim takes this new picture or desired state and changes the visual intensity of the picture. This includes making it brighter, making it bigger, changing the distance etc. Next he would bring back the old picture of the situation he wants to change and step into this picture. Tim must be fully associated with this old picture he wants to change. In the lower left-hand corner of this old picture, Tim would now insert a small, dark picture of the new desired state he wants. Now speed is critical as Tim would simultaneously take the picture of the current state and rapidly shrink it and allow it to become a distant point while the picture in the lower left corner is exploded into full view. At the time of this quick change an external or internal "swish" sound can be made if Tim wanted to. The key is to repeat this simultaneous picture swapping a minimum of five times. The intent is to install choices for a different way of doing a pattern. This particular method does not focus on changing or removing the old habit. Other techniques we will cover can help to achieve this. The point is to gain greater control over the triggers that are causing you to go into your habitual stress routines or scripts.

Measuring your energy and seeing the impact

The energy that you have can be measured, which makes managing your energy such an important focus area in your life. Dr. Konstantin Korotkov's book *Energy of Consciousness* covers what he calls Electrophotonics which provides the ability to see a person's human energy field. This also aids in the ability to detect imbalances and dysfunctions in the body. It works by using a software program where all ten fingers are measured. By using the principles of Chinese energy meridians, the fingers are associated with different organs and systems in the body. The ability to measure the human energy field allows you to understand better how such things as your stress levels impact your energy field. Seeing the results gives you added motivation to take steps to handle your stress better. The ability to measure and see your energy field provides an opportunity to manage your energy better.

The ability to measure beyond the individual energy fields and to measure an entire space or group of people is possible using a sensor device Dr. Korotkov has created called Sputnik. In February 2013, I participated in a five-day meditation workshop in Arizona where his device was positioned at the back of the stage and was measuring several parameters and the standard deviation of them every five seconds. The session had around 200 people in attendance and each session included a group meditation with music. The results were a steady increase in the energy every day over the five days. One day a noticeable decrease could be seen. This day was when the group meditation was focused on the past and the things people no longer wanted in their life. This was an amazing insight to observe, that the entire energy in the room decreased when the group was focusing and meditating on the negative. If this is happening on a group level, imagine what is happening with your energy when you are focused on the negative, past events and the things you no longer want in your life.

The book *There is a Spiritual Solution to Every Problem* by Dr. Wayne W. Dyer demonstrates the impact these negative thoughts have by using muscle testing. He uses the techniques from the book by Dr. David R. Hawkins *Power vs. Force: The Hidden Determinants of Human Behavior* to test. In one test he has the person think about the first time they were in love and their arm stayed strong and could not be pushed down as they had it extended. When he had the person think of a time they felt shame, their arm was easily able to be pushed down with minimal pressure. Just by thinking of shame the body weakens. An interesting test he also did was to have the person select an envelope that had a substance in it and had them hold it to their solar plexus while he muscle tested them. The person did not know what was in the envelopes. The envelope that had vitamin C in it tested strong, while with the one with aspartame, found in diet soft drinks, the muscle tested weak. The key point is that thought and what we ingest impacts our energy as demonstrated by these muscle tests.

Imagine what having a device like Sputnik and using muscle testing could do for better understanding your energy levels and the energy levels in your home, office, club or any environment. Being able to measure your individual or group energy levels will give you the ability to see the impacts on the energy and give you the ability to take actions to change your energy. Continuous monitoring will then demonstrate the impact that your actions have to achieve the results you want. Your energy fuels your transformation to become the conscious leader you want to be.

Key Points

Your takeaway from this chapter is your energy is the juice to fuel your personal transformation to live the life of your desire. We covered together:

- The three components of how your energy management and focus have an impact on your overall confidence, courage and taking bold action, plus unlocking your full potential.

- The six components and enabler to how to manage your energy system and exercises and questions to further your awareness of which areas are working in your life today and which areas need focus.

- The five tools and exercises to assist you in expanding your energy.

- The questions and examples to identify energy traps and steps you can take to avoid them.

CHAPTER 2

Limitations That Hold You From Your Greatness

Limitations and obstacles preventing you from achieving what you want

Sophie is a wonderful young lady who was underweight and had a challenge that impacted her ability to sleep every night. To add to her problem she could not sleep alone. Her obstacle was a result of her past. When she was eight years old her mother woke her up and said that her father was downstairs and was going to kill himself. Her mother needed her to go downstairs and talk him out of it. Here she was eight years old; her mother did not have the power to intervene and needed her to do it. All the weight was on her shoulders to save her father's life. This left her in a trauma that resulted in her being unable to sleep alone. The impact is she has had numerous partners and non-working relationships just to be able to sleep. This is an example of a personal limiter that was holding her back from achieving what she really wanted, which is the freedom to not hear screaming when she closed her eyes.

Tina needed to feed her baby with a syringe. One evening he began to choke and started turning blue. She tried many things to clear his passage with no luck. The emergency responders arrived and were able to resume normal breathing. Four years later every time her son begins to even sound like he has something in his throat she goes into panic and nearly passes out from the anxiety rush. In her words this puts her in a non-resourceful state that prevents her from responding to the situation. Instead this past limiter that she is still living with plays out every time she thinks her son is choking.

Marc is a striker for a professional Belgian soccer team. He had a clear breakaway during a critical match when the opposing goalie came out and toward him. Marc kicked the ball with his strong right foot and sent the ball past the goalie and over the top of the net. The emotions from the event that are playing in his subconscious impacted his play to where the next time he had the exact same situation, he repeated the same result and missed the goal. Some would say he is in a slump, just needs to snap out of it. He has a limiter that is impacting his play, and if not resolved will impact his career.

These three examples show a range of limitations that through an experience they had with a very heightened emotion created a pattern that is impacting their life and preventing them from achieving what they really want. A limiter is a belief, emotion, circumstance, habit or thought that is holding you back from achieving what you want. This could be just being free to go to sleep without needing to be with someone, not panicking when your child chokes or being able to hit the goal with the ball. In this chapter we are going to look at how you find what is limiting you from your greatness, the impact these limitations can have on your transformation and steps to minimize and overcome your limiters.

Finding your limitations to your greatness

I have highlighted that a limiter is a belief, emotion, circumstance, habit or thought that is holding you back from achieving what you want. Awareness becomes essential in helping you to identify what is holding you back and from what. You may not be seeing it yourself and this is where another person can help you find what is blocking you. Julie is a professional woman who asked if I could be her mentor to help her advance her career. Julie is respected as an expert in her area and as someone who connects very well with her company's partners when she works with them. In our first discussion I focused on two areas to identify what I could help her with. The first area was on her brand. I asked, "What is your brand and what feedback are you getting that supports this?" What I tend to find is people have their aspiration of what they want their brand to be and yet it does not match the feedback they are getting. Julie mentioned she was getting feedback she was hard to work with and she came across as being cold to people. This was great feedback to start digging deeper into the subject on what was causing this feedback. After clarifying and getting examples of where this could be true in her job, I then asked, "Is this how you are with your family and friends?" She answered no; her family and friends see her as being very open and warm to them. This was painting a picture that she was not being congruent with her personal and professional life. In asking more questions around this difference the awareness she needed became clearer to her. She was holding a belief that for a woman to succeed in the corporate world she had to be hard, cold and distant. This matched the feedback she was getting and did not match who she really was. The important factor is she now was aware of the belief she was holding and this is what was needed to help her make different choices. Different choices will then lead to different outcomes.

The second area Julie and I focused on was around "What do you want to be famous for?" This question is to help you identify what you want people to be calling you for. What type of jobs do you want people to be thinking of you about and reach out to see if you are interested? This helps you determine your limiters, by matching what you think you are good at to what others think you are good at. Julie came up with areas where she thought she was very good. To validate her view with others, she asked 10 people she knew in different capacities to be very open and provide her with two things the person believes she does really well and two things she could improve on. In addition, Julie did a follow-up discussion with each person to help her understand the feedback. Yes, this takes courage from Julie to do and the exercise is extremely beneficial in helping you identify your potential blind spots. Those limiters you may not be aware of yet. If you can have a trusting and open feedback session while doing this, without judging or being your own worst critic, you will get information that will go beyond the coffee side chat type of feedback. What I mean by coffee side chat type feedback is where you get feedback that says you need to work on your communication, influence, persuasion and similar soft skills. These soft skills all have a benefit and focusing on these will help you improve your performance. However, they just will not hit the mark on what is really holding you back that managers and peers are not that good in understanding, even though they sense it, and will rarely ever tell you. For example, one piece of feedback Julie received was that she made decisions impacting her team and herself, because of her strong need to please people. The feedback came with timely examples, which helped her to realize how this belief pattern was impacting her performance. She was struggling with authentic communication to her stakeholders and made workarounds that impacted her team and her leaders' perception of her. This is the rare honest feedback that is pure gold to give a person the awareness to go after it.

In addition to the questions above, the following exercises are an aid to help you find your limiters, so that once you are aware and make different decisions and choices will lead to different outcomes in your life.

◕ Exercise: What keeps showing up in your life?

From the work in the energy chapter you captured a number of items in the exercises that drain your energy. Use this list as a starting point or just start to journal on what are common themes and emotions that are showing up in your life. As you journal and capture these, ask the following questions:

- What emotions or themes do you regularly have in your life? For example, you may have anger as something that comes up regularly, or you may find you are constantly worried about money, people show up in your life and they all behave the same to you. Whatever these are, record them in your journal.

- What is the cause of this emotion or theme?

- What are examples of these situations that cause the emotion or theme to begin?

- How do these make you feel?

◕ Exercise: Mapping your thoughts, patterns and emotions.

An analytical tool that I find helps me is to create a connect map of emotions, situations and themes that are consistently coming up to see if there is a connection. This is meant to give better awareness of whether this is a standalone event or if I feel it is connected with something else that has occurred in my life. Using the work from what drains your energy or the exercise above, map any connections that you are finding with the emotions, events or themes in your life, like the example below.

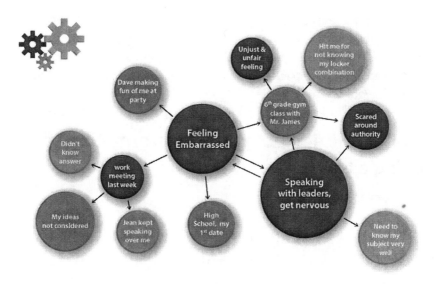

🎯 Exercise: Which themes do you resonate with?

From the themes listed below, circle the ones you resonate with the most. These are potential themes that are common in your life and consuming a lot of your energy and limiting you from your own greatness. If you do not resonate with any of these, what themes do you feel are commonly showing up in your life?

Caretaker	Searcher	Dreamer	Mercenary
Your drive is helping people and you put other people's needs before your own.	You are constantly seeking in your life for the next relationship, thing, promotion or other to find fulfillment in your life.	You have constant ideas on what you & others can do, yet you never bring them to reality by taking action.	You chase any cause or pursue any activity as you get paid for it, or it directly benefits you.
Justice	**Pleaser**	**Avoider**	**Perfection**
Everything must equal justice based on your definition of what is the high ground for any situation.	You are compelled to please other people even if you do not want to or do not even like them.	You will go out of your way to avoid making decisions or taking action that will benefit you or change your situation.	Everything you do must be perfect & this consumes a lot of your time & energy.
Complainer	**Victim**	**One Better**	**Gossiper**
It is hard to find satisfaction in any situation as you can always find faults to complain about.	You may believe the world is out to get you as you are a victim & it is never your fault.	Whatever anyone else has done you always have done something better & will highlight it in conversations.	You spend a lot of your time talking about others behind their back.
Fire Fighter	**Know it All**	**Judger**	**Jealous**
You go from one crisis to another in your life & if there is no crisis you create one.	You have all the answers & no one can tell you anything you do not know already.	You live very high standards you created & it is difficult for anyone to live up to them without your judgment.	You are envious/resentful of someone's achievements, possessions, or etc. they have & you don't.

These methods are just some ideas on how you can identify the limiters that are holding you back from your greatness. In the next section you will become more aware of how these limiters are impacting you and holding you back from your transformation of making conscious leadership in action in your life

Limitations impact your transformation and being a leader

People tend to fail for five reasons:

1. They do not have a compelling enough reason or purpose.

2. Their beliefs are limiting them.

3. They do not manage their energy well.

4. They will never act in a way that is inconsistent with their own identity, which is the way they see themselves. The exercise on identifying themes in your life above is an example. If someone's identity is being a complainer, without making a change in their life they will be consistent with being a complainer.

5. They do not have an environment that supports them. You will be like the people you spend the majority of your time with.

Limiters tend to contribute to many of these five failure modes. Limiters can also impact you in a number of different ways professionally, personally and can even make you ill. In the previous section Julie's belief that a woman in a corporate environment must be hard was holding her career back as the feedback on her behavior and performance matched her belief. The behavior was not congruent with how she lives her life, so this mismatch was also not making her happy with her overall life. As we covered in the managing your energy chapter, one area in your life can drain all the other areas and impact your entire life. In Julie's case this one belief was impacting her both professionally and personally.

Dirk's limiters almost stopped him from taking a new job opportunity, because he was unaware that the concerns he was having about the new role were related to his beliefs. Dirk had contacted me to discuss the opportunity. I have worked with him in the past and we have known each other for the last six years. As we have a very good level of trust in our relationship, I was able to ask questions around his concerns about taking the new job opportunity. Dirk raised two points: the team was all located in one city except for him and the team was mostly engineers and he was not. Both of these can be sound reasons for not taking the position. The role was something he really wanted, was the most logical career move for him to advance his knowledge, make a difference with his experience they required, as well as give him a better chance for promotion. It was a great opportunity. The beliefs that were in play were around trust and connections. These are so strong that he was ready to decline the role. By becoming aware of these beliefs, he was able to make a different choice and this led to a different outcome. We discussed options to build the trust and relationships that would create what he desired. Dirk implemented the actions, felt comfortable and took the opportunity. It has worked out well and he enjoys being in the new team and the new job.

Beliefs and decisions we make around them can become key limiters that impact your success. Sandy is a professional coach and her beliefs around money and asking for money for her services prevents her from making a comfortable living by helping others. Phillip who is also a professional coach was not following up with his client list, newsletter or webpage. His business was just surviving until he became aware that when he was 22 he had a significant event in his life where while studying law he was asked to present a paper he had submitted to the entire class. The issue was he borrowed the paper from his roommate and did not know it well enough to present it in front of the professor and class. This was naturally embarrassing and he was caught doing something he would probably do differently today. This incident created a trauma experience for him when it occurred and what was more important was the decision he made to himself at that time, which was it does not matter what you do, there is no reason to try. This belief that was created that day was still impacting him 26 years later and he did not even know it, until he became aware of it. This "no reason to try" belief was working in his subconscious every day of his life. Awareness is a very powerful tool to help you understand how your limiters are impacting the life you want to live.

Jean's stress had caused her to become ill and she had to take off two and a half months from work to recover. Jean was under a lot of stress at work and had a number of projects she was responsible for to ensure they were in good order before going on vacation. She was working extra hard to make sure they were all handed over properly to her co-workers. The day she was to go on vacation she developed fibromyalgia, which is a condition that causes pain in the muscles, tendons and ligaments in her shoulder and arm. She could not sit up in a chair nor could she use a computer to work. She rested and did physical therapy to be able to go back to work. The interesting point is when Jean returned to work, she started working with a coach using Emotional Freedom Techniques (EFT), which was founded by Gary Craig (http://www.eftuniverse.com/). EFT helped Jean to release the negative energy and emotions tied to events throughout her life. Each situation where the emotions were released allowed her to learn new things about those events. This included what beliefs and perceptions she had formed around those episodes. The real interesting thing is as she started the work on herself her subconscious began showing her more and more pictures of moments in her life to gain relief and emotional freedom from. This gave her awareness and techniques to not only identify the situations and beliefs in her life, but also provided a method to overcoming the emotion around them. This has led to five years free of another incident of fibromyalgia.

These examples above highlight how individual beliefs can impact you. There are also socially common held beliefs, family beliefs and organizational beliefs that can also impact. A sports example was the commonly held social belief before May 6, 1954 that it was humanly impossible for someone to break the four-minute mile mark, until Roger Bannister did it that day. Once this belief was proven to not be true, within six weeks Roger's record was broken. This story also gives a clue to how to change beliefs. Demonstrate that it is not true by seeking proof or designing your own experiments to disprove the components that make up your belief.

In the above examples, an essential element is awareness of what beliefs are being factors that are limiting you from your greatness. How do you know limiters are impacting your life? When something is coming up like a feeling around an event, person etc., ask yourself: to feel this way what do I have to believe? This will begin to give you insight into your beliefs. How about if your identity is a factor? One way is to look at different scenarios in your life. For example, say you are in a difficult conversation and you feel strong emotions coming up as the conversation plays out. You may feel as though you are being knocked off your balance. Ask yourself and journal on the following questions:

- What do I consider to be my identity? For example, Fred who leads a team of 16 people found that his identity was he needed to know all the answers to feel competent. In a team meeting he would start to be asked a number of questions he did not know the answer to and he felt a lot of emotion come up. This led to a performance impact on his team as he would not communicate on things he was not 100% certain he knew the answers to. Thus his identity of having to know the answers to be competent was impacting his success.

- What feels at risk to me?

- How would I feel if what I fear is true?

- What am I really afraid of?

- What is the downside?

Limiters impact your ability to be the leader of your conscious transformation and impact the success you want to have in your life. In the next section we discuss what you can do to minimize and overcome your limitations.

Steps to minimize and overcome your limitations

Where do you start to overcome your limiters and how do you do it? Taiichi Ohno, famed for the Toyota production system quote, is very relevant to our subject, "Ask what the greatest point of need for improvement is and start from there." If you have been completing the exercises along the way you will have a list of the items you are now aware of to work on, or just by being aware of them you can make different decisions or choices and this will lead to different outcomes. The starting point is to understand the situation and the limiter you want to focus on first. In the following exercise, you will answer the questions to help you understand what you would like to be doing and the reason why and also what are you doing instead of what you want to be doing and why. To further your understanding I will provide two examples of when I did this exercise with others with each question.

- Think about what you would like to be doing more of in your life. Write down what you would like to spend more of your time on. Andrea said she would like to be spending more time with her children and on her art. She is a painter with a family and has two younger school-aged children. Keaton is a director for a high-tech organization, he said he wanted to spend more time planning.

- When you look at what you have written down, ask yourself why you would like to be doing this. This is to understand your motivation and what gain do you believe this will give you. Andrea mentioned she loves spending time with her children and feels creative when she can paint. For her the gain was feeling more connected with her children and being creative. For Keaton, he wanted to work on his team's vision and provide greater strategic direction to his organization. He wanted to be more proactive with the gain of having more control over the outcomes his team is involved with. Keaton felt he was living each day in a reactive mode.

- Rather than doing what you want to do from how you answered the question above, what are you doing instead? The purpose of this question is to understand what you are spending your time on doing, instead of what you want to be doing. Andrea highlighted she ends up daily spending time cleaning their family's home and doing daily chores in the house. She sees a mess and is compelled to clean it up and will be distracted until she completes it. Keaton spends his time firefighting issues and escalations all day long. He finds himself sitting behind his desk and being tied to his email to respond quickly to anything that comes in.

- Why are you doing this activity and what is the gain that you get from it? This question helps to gain an understanding of the motivation and drive that makes you spend time on it. You are getting something from this and thus this is why you are doing it. Andrea got the feeling the house was always ready to entertain people and was always looking well maintained. She perceived her mother-in-law and husband had the expectation of her that the house has to always be in perfect order. The gain was to please them and by doing so she would then be accepted and this ultimately means being loved. Keaton felt indispensable and his reputation was he was always quick to respond and be on top of all escalations. His gain was this is the key to his recognition, brand

and feeling valuable. Hopefully you can start to see what beliefs they have around this situation and the motivation that compels them to do what they are doing and not what they want to be doing. This is critical to be aware of the gain you are getting by doing the behavior you are doing, instead of the behavior you want to be doing. The gain is what reinforces why you do it. It is the magnet that draws you to repeating the behavior over and over again.

- People tend to have fantasies about the worst thing that can happen in a given situation. What is the worst case that could happen if you stopped doing the behavior you are currently doing, instead of the activity you want to be doing? This helps you to think through what could be the worst case situation if you did stop doing this activity. Andrea thought the worst case would be her husband would leave and divorce her if she did not keep the house clean. Keaton believed the worst case was he would not be considered indispensable and could be replaced. He also felt his brand would be impacted as he would not be as responsive to answer his emails quickly.

- What can you do to determine if your worst-case situation is true or not? Is there an experiment that you can do to test your belief? One method to overcome a belief is to have evidence that shows you it is not true. A way to do this is design an experiment so you can test this belief. Andrea planned to experiment with not always having the house 100% clean at all times and to schedule and follow through with spending time with her children and painting. Keaton started to let his team members handle the escalations more and more by themselves. His intent was also to empower them at the same time to resolve the issues. As I followed up with him, he said at first people were asking, "What is wrong, why are you slow with answering?" He resisted reverting back to his old patterns to test his experiment.

The following are other steps you can use to minimize and overcome your limiters:

- ***Are you in a failing situation?*** Your limiter could be you are in a no-win situation and you do not even know it. These situations are more difficult to determine. Hans was a director of operations and while working for the previous vice president, his career was tracking and he was viewed as being a strong leader in his area of focus. When the new vice president came in to lead the organization, Hans continued to do what he did for his old vice president, believing this strategy worked in the past so it should work again. The problem is it did not and Hans did not see it or even become aware of it. His limiter was his attitude and approach of not getting to know what was important to his new leader and not building rapport with him. He did not adjust his way of working and Hans was managed out from his company and never understood what really happened. During an acquisition, some members from the acquired company took on the belief that I will just keep my head down, work hard on what I know and not worry about integrating or learning about my new company. Within two years these same people were let go from their new company.

These are two examples where the individuals had fallen into a no-win situation that they caused and did not know it. Being aware is a key first step. In a working environment, if you perceive things are not going well and the feedback is contrary to your views, get more feedback. Either you can get it directly from your leader, a close peer, a colleague or use the technique we discussed earlier where you ask 10 people for feedback on two things going well and two things that you can work on. View the feedback as a gift and look closely at what you get to determine the wisdom you can gain from the feedback. Then make choices from this new level of understanding to minimize or overcome the limiter. You will need to change in order to see a change in them. Expecting others to change and you do not will result, as in these two examples, in being let go or passed up for greater opportunities.

- *Journaling to dissect and understand.* Journaling gives you an opportunity to have a dialog with yourself and capture thoughts and things you would like to see more of in your life. For example, if you want more gratitude in your life, then each day capture three to five things you are grateful for. Where you put your focus, your energy will flow. In addition, your journal gives you a great place to dissect and understand the limiter that you want to work on.

We have covered a number of questions already that you can use, such as:

- o What belief is causing me to feel this way?

- o What am I really afraid of about this situation?

- o What about this situation makes me feel this way?

- o What else could it mean?

- o What actions can I take to limit this or change it?

- **_Take action._** The best way to start building your willpower muscle is to take action and follow through. At the moment of a new idea, goal or direction, instantly take some sort of action toward its achievement. This could be ordering a new book, making an appointment with a coach, brainstorming an action plan or anything that will start you on the path to take action. The second part is to make it stick by doing it for at least the next 28 days straight to make your new goal and commitment a habit. It is critical to stick with it to make it part of your success routine. The purpose of this exercise is to make a commitment, take some sort of action immediately and do it 28 straight days to make it part of what you do.

  - o Take one of your limiters identified and journal on what three commitments you will achieve in the next six months.

  - o Next to each of your commitments, list your outcome, purpose and action steps you will take to make this happen.

  - o Pick one of them now and do it.

  - o Now make your dreams come true by doing the things you want to be part of your daily success routine for the next 28 days. Make them fun to do and enjoy doing them. A way to look at it is you are building a success routine to change your life the way you want it to be. Let this inspire you.

- **_Make your calendar your best friend._** What gets scheduled is what gets accomplished. To overcome a limiter your calendar becomes your friend by scheduling the actions you will be taking from the exercise above. It all comes down to making the time, doing it and achieving anything. You may find you have beliefs about time that will need to be worked on as one of your limiters. If you find yourself saying you do not have time to do this or you are too busy to do something, then this is a great area to start with to dissect your beliefs about time. A technique I find helpful is from Robin Sharma's audio program and workbook *Manage Your Time, Master Your Life.* This provides a great process to plan my week. How I use it is first I review the plan from the week before and look for the lessons I learned. Reflection is important to gain the wisdom of what works well and doesn't work for me. I then review my planning book I made in this order: my vision board (all those pictures and words of what I want to achieve in my life); my 14 intentions of what I want to achieve before I die; my commitments (my purpose statement and code of conduct); my life plan (four personal and four professional categories); long-term goal chart (three bullets for personal and professional goals for one, three, five and 10 years); and finally my 90-day goals for personal and professional categories. This creates focus on what I need to do to achieve what is most important to me. Next I plan out my week and the goals I want to achieve. For each goal I structure them to ensure I am extremely clear on what I want as my outcome, why I want it and what actions I will take to achieve it. I also add how this will make me feel. Adding emotion gives the goal energy to fuel me achieving it. The next step is very important. I then schedule my activities in my calendar to support my weekly plan. I then do a daily brief review of my weekly plan to keep my focus and energy flowing to those most life-important goals to me.

A second technique around time and the beliefs you may have around not having enough time is to change your language. If you catch yourself saying "I do not have enough time to do that" or something similar, change your language. A start is by saying "I do not have enough time yet to do that." The "yet" is powerful as it gives you the belief that it will be possible to have more time. Ultimately you will want to remove the language from your dialog and this will give you freedom from putting pressure on yourself about time.

These are a few steps you can use to help you minimize and overcome your limiters. Some of your limiters will require deeper focus to overcome and I will share additional techniques later in the book.

Key Points

Your takeaway from this chapter is your limitations can hold you from achieving your greatness to live the life of your desire. We covered together:

- How to go about finding your limitations with exercises on what keeps showing up in your life; mapping your thoughts, patterns and emotions; and which items resonate with you most.

- How limitations impact your conscious transformation and being the leader of your transformation. This included the four reasons people fail and examples to reinforce the lessons.

- Tools and exercises to assist you in minimizing and overcoming your limiters.

CHAPTER 3

Tools That Drive Your Transformation

Tools can help you drive your transformation – start with your story

"Take the first step in faith. You don't have to see the whole staircase. Just take the first step." – Dr. Martin Luther King, Jr.

Beginning your conscious transformation is like taking your first step. Your transformation may have started from a number of different situations that have happened in your life. One may be a traumatic event or a decision you have made that you want something else in your life. You may not be happy with what is currently happening in your work life, relationship or personal life. However you have come to start your journey, there are a number of tools that can help you along the way. In this chapter you will learn about the different tools that will aid you along your journey. The beginning is to understand your story and use this as a guide, a badge of inspiration, a means to drive your motivation on why your transformation is important to you. When I say story, this not about how you have been a victim and the universe is out to get you. This is an uplifting story that gives you that desire in the darkest hours to continue with changing your life to get what you want most from your life. Your story is your game-changing event or events that give you inspiration to be the best you can be every day.

First, I would like to share the game-changing event that started my journey to give you an example to help you look into your life and find what your catalyst for your change is. In everyone's life there are one or many opportunities, challenges or situations that become a game-changing event in a person's life. In Elise Ballard's book *Epiphany* she provides a vehicle for many people to tell their stories about the key event that changed their life. She defines an epiphany as, "a moment of great or sudden revelation; an intuitive grasp of reality through something unusually simple and striking; an illuminating discovery, realization, or disclosure." When each of us looks at our life and focuses on what moments made a difference, we will find our own epiphany. My story occurred in the war in Iraq during Operation Desert Storm. It became my life-changing event that has taken me on an amazing journey.

Iraq - Day 3 of the ground offensive of Operation Desert Storm (Tuesday February 26, 1991). I was a first lieutenant with Bravo Company, an infantry unit, and I was the organization's executive officer. Since the ground offensive began we were constantly on the move and in frequent engagement with Iraqi forces. On this particular day we were fighting against the Iraqi Republican Guard and this day would have a profound impact on my life and the future direction I would follow.

From night to day was a blur and the sky was black from the burning oil well fires. My company was deployed on line and firing at targets to our front and all around us. I remember the ground being littered with destroyed equipment and ammunition. The sounds of explosions and the firing of weapons were happening in every direction around me. I could see my company commander's vehicle off to my left as my vehicle started up an incline, when Castro my driver yelled out, "Sniper ahead!" The sniper had my commander in his line of fire when I first saw him. I instantly began to push down on my firing trigger to take him out. At this moment he turned and we were both staring directly at each other. It was as if the world stopped moving. A tunnel encapsulated us both and everything was moving in slow motion. It felt as though I was watching an old Western gunfight scene, except I was in it and this was a matter of life and death. Without hesitation there was no play left in my trigger and I was squeezing the last bit of pressure needed to complete the task. With our eyes locked on each other, he did something I did not expect. He threw his weapon to the ground, went to his knees and began to pray out loud to Allah. My finger released the grip I had on my trigger. Neither of us was to die at that moment in time.

Castro covered me and kept his weapon aimed on this man who was now lying on the ground as I jumped out of our vehicle and went to get the other four Iraqi soldiers out of their fighting position. Soon the five men were lying on the ground as I started to check each one for weapons.

When I was checking one of the men I made the fatal type of mistake. Soldiers are trained to search prisoners of war by lying on the ground next to them and reaching over and searching them from behind. The reason is if they are booby-trapped with an explosive device we can roll them on top of it and hopefully not kill ourselves in the process. As I was checking the man with whom just a few minutes ago I was in a mortal stare down, I felt something next to his chest that did not feel right. Rather than rolling him on top of it, I pulled it out and saw a black cylinder tube with wires coming out of the top and heard a distinct sound I knew very well, a thud. This was the sound of a round or charge going down a tube to hit a firing pin. My body completely shut down and I said to myself I'm dead.

I have heard stories that when you know you are about to die your life flashes before your eyes. This was completely true for me. As I truly believed I was dead from the critical mistake I had just made, I saw my life in an instant flash before my eyes. I saw images of all the important people in my life from my grandparents, parents, great friends I had, my partner Ellen and an image of a small blond-haired boy about four years old. At that time Ellen was pregnant and we did not know the sex of our first child. That image I saw would be Eric, our firstborn son, and he would look exactly as I had pictured him that day in a flash of my life. All the images I saw were of people who were at their happiest moment. There were no pictures of possessions or things I have accomplished. I just simply saw key people who shared my life and one who would be in my life. I did not fully realize the gift I had just been given. This gift would transform my life forever. No I was not dead. The device I had pulled out of his jacket was a homemade radio and the sound I heard was batteries sliding down the tube. This was what we called in the army a shorts changing moment.

This was the situation, however what was my epiphany? Seeing my life flash before my eyes was all about the great people in my life, not the titles, cars, things etc. The wisdom I gained was to start from the end of your life in mind and be the best person I could be by helping others. The questions I began to ask myself and journal on were: What is the legacy I want to leave? What would I like my obituary to say about how I showed up in life? What are the important things I want to achieve? This was a powerful experience to ground me clearly in what I wanted to become, act and be every day. This launched me on my journey to put people first, live life to the fullest, follow my soul's intent and have fun learning new and wonderful things. Your story therefore includes two parts: the situation that happened and the wisdom you gained from it. For me the actions that happened that day on the battlefield and what I had seen when I was convinced I was about to die and the wisdom I gained from seeing my life flash before my eyes makes up my story. The lessons you gain are the secret sauce to your story and become the driving agent to create the change you want to be. Without this learning I would just be literally telling you another war story.

Now is your opportunity to find your epiphany and story that will be your inspiration along your path of changing to achieve the life you want. What is that moment in your life that has sparked your transformation? As reading a book is a conversation you have with the author, journaling is a conversation with yourself. The purpose of this exercise is to begin your habit of taking time daily to think about your story, your successes and all the other great things that you want to manifest into your life. What you focus on is where your energy flows. Your action: if you do not already have a journal, go out and get one. Use your journal to be your transformation tool to help you make the changes you want in your life. Spend at least 10 minutes a day and go deep within yourself and answer these questions:

- What is my epiphany (game-changing event)?

- What wisdom can I gain from this game-changing moment?

- What are my gifts?

- What legacy do I want to leave?

- What three actions can I take today that will bring me closer to the legacy I want to leave?

The power of using tools

Tools, techniques, guides, devices and a whole list of other aids are meant to help you make what you are trying to achieve easier. If you are learning a new sport you may start by reading about how to do it, watching a DVD or friend do it, you may take lessons from a coach, go to a practice range, and buy equipment and training aids to help you get better at it and many other things. The steps that you take are designed to make you more proficient at doing it and move you toward mastery. The same holds true for driving the transformation and change that you want to make in your life. Tools assist by giving you more confidence to build supportive habits for sustaining your journey and change you want. For example, Kepner-Trego is a company that offers analytical troubleshooting as a tool to help you to use questioning to narrow down to the most likely reason something has caused an issue, before you physically go and take an action. This makes sense as if you are at the stage to do something physically to attempt to resolve the issue, the action will take time and cost money to complete the activity. In the Belgium Cisco's Technical Assistant Center (TAC), I was part of training our TAC engineers on how to use this technique to resolve customer issues when they called in. After one of these training sessions which lasted for four days, that Saturday one of the engineers who was trained that week found himself on the phone with a large customer who had what was referred to as a network down situation. This means they have a server issue impacting their network, costing revenue and time by not being fully operational. The engineer was not an expert in the area the customer had an issue with and he was feeling the pressure to get this up and running as soon as possible. The engineer used the analytical troubleshooting tool he just learned that week and through questions was able to find the cause and suggest a fix. He resolved the issue within 30 minutes and said the tool gave him the confidence he needed to tackle it. This is what the different tools we will be covering will help you with; giving you more confidence to tackle issues and guide you along your transformation.

Tools are powerful as they help you to be yourself. Finding your true inner self requires you to do the daily work with yourself. It is essential for each of us to focus on our inner self to make the changes we want to have in our life. If you want the world to change, you need to change the words you use and the thoughts you have first. Why is this so critical to master? In her book *You Can Heal Your Life* Louise L. Hay states, "If we are willing to do the mental work, almost anything can be healed." The message this wonderful book provides is that we are each responsible for our own reality and "dis-ease." Her belief is we are making ourselves ill when we have thoughts of self-hatred. Tools help you with the inner work to achieve the change and the more you use and master the tool, the more the changes become a natural part of you

Practicing with the tools and techniques helps you to become more proficient at using them. Practice and rehearsals are an absolute must on your list of items to add to your toolkit. This is powerful in helping to build the success routines that will sustain you along your journey. This works by the three steps of learn, apply and build the habit. Practicing reinforces the application of what you have been learning from your readings, journal, questions you are asking yourself, seminars, and classes. The more you apply and practice, the more you create the habit of making this part of your daily actions that occur subconsciously without you having to put much conscious thought into it.

In the U.S. military practice and rehearsals are an essential part of preparing for missions to help make the steps you need to take automatic in the most challenging situations. As a military leader you are taught the eight troop leading procedures for preparing for operations, and under the supervision step you have rehearsing as one of the key elements. The eight steps include: Receive the mission, Issue a warning order, Make a tentative plan, Start necessary movement, Reconnoiter, Complete the plan, Issue the complete order and Supervise. Rehearsals help to improve performance by practicing the important elements to be achieved, build confidence by allowing your team to understand better how the operation will be executed and assist in identifying weaknesses in the plan.

From my earlier story about being in Desert Storm when I went to get the other four Iraqi soldiers out of their fighting position, I was operating with limited sleep and the intelligence we had was the Iraqi military was booby-trapping their equipment and fighting positions. At this time I was running on adrenalin and instinct. The instinct was based on the training and practicing of basic skills I had done over and over again. Without thought before entering the fighting position I started checking for trip wires, just as I was trained and practiced. This was powerful as the knowledge I acquired was being used when I needed it most to protect my life. The point is practice and rehearsing will help you master the tools and skills you want to acquire to aid in your change process.

What tools can you use for your transformation?

With your personal transformation story completed from the exercise you have completed in your journal you hopefully have already acquired, you will want to know what tools or techniques you can use to help you with your transformation. When and what tool you should use will be covered in the next sections. In this section you will get an understanding of the types of tools that are available, what they can help you with, and a description and resource guide to gain more information. This table highlights the tools we will cover.

Tools	Description
Life Plan & Vision Statement	Define what you want by creating your picture of what success means to you.
Vision Board	Visually reinforce what you want to achieve by collecting & displaying pictures that best represent what you want in your life.
Affirmations	Positive statements that you repeat often to shift your beliefs.
80/20 Rule	20% of the actions you take create 80% of the results. Your goal is to find the 20%.
Adopt a Responsible Mind-set	Change your victim story by becoming responsible for what you get in your life.
Emotional Freedom Technique (EFT & Matrix Reimprinting	Release the emotions & beliefs that are part of your past that you are still living every day.
Meditation	Reduce stress & relax while living in the present moment.

The tools selected are meant to help you with three steps for your success of becoming aware, which allows you to make better choices and this leads to different results being achieved. You then just need to observe if you are getting the results you want and if not change again until you do. I encourage you to try out the ones that feel right to you and build your own success routines. This is how you will put all of the things together that you are learning in this book and help you achieve your own amazing success.

🌀 Tool: Life plan and vision statement

Creating your life plan and vision statement is a tool to help define what you really want. Together they inspire, energize and help you to create a picture of your desired outcomes. They will act as your guide and be a driving force to keep you on your path of what you want to accomplish. The first step is to define your personal vision statement. To achieve this, answer the following questions:

- What does success look like to you?

- What do you want to accomplish in the future?

- What is your purpose?

- What are your values?

Once you have finished answering the questions, look at what you have written and now build a personal, memorable, easy to understand and meaningful vision for yourself. The statement is best to be for the next three to five years. Another way to look at it is this is your direction statement of where you are heading on your journey and what you want to be. There is no right or wrong vision statement, so no judgment and have fun with creating it.

With your vision statement complete, your life plan is the essence of how you are going to achieve your vision. It includes your strategy or those major areas you are going to focus on to achieve it, your reason why you want to achieve it and your goals or actions that are going to make it happen. A way to look at your strategy can be to review the six components and the one enabler to how to manage your energy system we discussed in Chapter 1. They included: relations and connections; focus; being in spirit; release – physical – nutrition; occupation – living your life purpose; beliefs and emotional health; and network and support. For example, you could select as one of your strategies that you want to be in great physical condition. You would then ask yourself why you want to achieve this, which is your purpose. As mentioned before, one reason people fail is they do not have a compelling enough reason. Then you will capture the goals or actions that will help you achieve your strategy. Your goals should follow the format of being SMART: Specific, Measurable, Attainable, Realistic and Time-bound. Here is how it could look like using the physical example:

Strategy: To be in great physical condition by December 31, 2016.

My reason why: To feel and be my best. To achieve my goals and be my best at work and when I'm with my family, I need great energy and being in great shape and exercising will give me this. I will look and feel amazing. I will have fun getting and being in amazing shape.

Goals to achieve my strategy:
- Run four times a week for 45 minutes on Monday, Wednesday, Friday and Sunday.

- Bike every other Saturday for one and a half hours from April 1 to September 15.

- Run the Brussels Half Marathon on October 8 and beat 1:50 for my time.

Before moving on, I want to address that some people have fears around setting goals. When some people look at longer-term goals they put it off because they do not know what they really want. They are afraid to commit to something if they don't know if they really want it. It could be they feel the goal is not lofty enough, their belief could be for five- to 10-year goals they need to be something Gandhi or Mother Teresa would achieve and again they put it off. Do this exercise to reveal any subconscious concerns to attaining the goal you have captured in your plan. Address them and do not let it subconsciously derail your achievement of it. Ask yourself:

- What is the worst thing that can happen if I achieve this goal?

- What is the next worst thing that could happen?

Continue doing this until you have brought up all the concerns and now that you are aware, let the concerns go.

With no concerns, and as already discussed, once you have a goal created, take action immediately to build momentum to achieving what you desire. In the example above, this can be going to your calendar, scheduling your training time and blocking this time out. What gets scheduled gets done and propels you to achieving the strategic component you selected.

Additional resources: Audio programs and workbook: *Manage Your Time, Master Your Life* – Robin Sharma; *Time of Your Life - 3 Ways to Take Control of Your Life* – Anthony Robbins.

𝒆 Tool: Vision boards.

Vision boards help you to reinforce visually what you want to achieve, be, and have in your life. It drives your focus. The power in your mind then helps you as it is searching for where your focus is in your environment. If you became aware of the Mini as we just came off the car dealer's lot, you will start to see Minis everywhere, where before they were not passing through your filters and now they are. This is the concept of how the vision board can help you with your transformation. You will build a vision board with pictures of what you want and review your vision board when you first wake up in the morning and before going to bed. Why these are key times is this is the window between your subconscious and conscious mind. This is that moment from when you are just waking up and when you are just getting ready to go to sleep. Your images on your vision board become imprinted in your subconscious and approximately 95% of what we do daily is subconscious routines and habits. Your subconscious works for you in helping to get what you really want.

To build your vision board, review your vision statement and life plan you have just created on what you want to achieve. Now find pictures from magazines, your photos or others that most represent what you want to achieve. A good friend Margie showed me that she had a picture of a bride and groom in a wedding scene and a picture of a newborn child on her vision board. These pictures represented something really important that she wanted in her life and when she showed me her vision board, she was already just married and now pregnant with their first child. She had created the vision board two and half years earlier and was now seeing the results in her life.

On my vision board for 2012 I had pictures that represented running the Chicago Marathon, traveling to Alaska, getting promoted and supporting Habitat for Humanity in giving back to charity. I had created my vision board at the end of 2011 for the next year and all four of these worked out and were achieved, because I was focused and reviewed my board twice a day and became aware of opportunities. One of these opportunities was to be part of a team doing a housing build project for Habitat for Humanity in Anchorage, Alaska with my oldest son. Doing the event with my son was an added bonus and having pictures of my family as part of my vision board helps me to continue my focus on how I want our relationship to evolve. The action is to cut out the pictures that represent what you want and arrange and attach them to your vision board. Then begin reviewing and visualizing your vision board first thing in the morning as you wake and just prior to going to bed.

Additional resources: Book: *Vision Board* – Joyce Schwarz.

🕑 Tool: Affirmations.

An affirmation is a tool for focus on what you want and want to change in your life. It works on your beliefs, as what you believe about yourself and your life is what you will have more of in your life. Henry Ford's quote highlights the importance of how your beliefs will impact your life when he said, "Whether you think you can, or you think you can't, you're right."

Your objective is to create affirmations that will transform your thoughts to have the characteristics you want to be and attract into your daily life. The key is to make your affirmations positive and not based on a negative. You then say your affirmations many times throughout the day and stick with them. Louise L. Hay expresses this with her Power Thought Cards, when she says, "Affirmations are like planting seeds in the ground. It takes some time to go from a seed to a full-grown plant. And so it is with affirmations – it takes some time from the first declaration to the final demonstration. So be patient."

In the beliefs and emotions part of the energy management section, I provided an example of when my boss at that time had asked me to consider two critical questions: "Do I want it?" and "Do I feel worthy?" The affirmation I created and still use today is a simple "I am enough." I play with this and have fun with it by making up songs when I'm running using this as the chorus. Your affirmation you create can be as simple or have more to it. Here are two more examples from two people who are very good at creating affirmations:

- "I lovingly do everything I can to assist my body in maintaining perfect health." Louise L. Hay

- "All I need is within me now and I have the courage to see it through." Tony Robbins

Additional resources: Book and cards: *You Can Heal Your Life* – Louise L. Hay; *Power Thought Cards* – Louise L. Hay; Workshop: Unleash the Power Within with Tony Robbins.

✪ Tool: 80/20 rule.

Pareto's 80/20 rule, otherwise called the Pareto principle, states that approximately 80% of the effects will come from 20% of the causes. As a transformation tool this helps you to be aware that 80% of your results will come from 20% of your actions. In leadership this comes down to 20% of your people in your organization will be driving 80% of your team's results. This means you need to play the numbers and take a lot of action and observe which actions are giving you the results you want in your life and stop the ones that are not working. The key for this tool to help you best is to measure, track and trend the results to the actions you are taking. One technique to assist you is to plot the changes you implement on a timeline and measure amount of changes over time. This also means you need to have a benchmark of where you are at today. You may also find that a combination of two or more changes results in the change you are looking for.

Another method to help you identify the actions that are creating the results you want is to keep a log. I do this for my running and I track the date, time ran, outside temperature, conditions, distance, route and notes of anything special about that training session. This could be feeling pain in an area or some before or after training session routine that worked well. I then can trend or review my training to see what is giving me my best results. This has been a big help in understanding what was happening before an injury occurred, so I can make changes to prevent the same injury from reoccurring in the future. You can use any means to track and measure your results and the important point is to find what actions are giving you the 80% of your results you want to build your awareness, and focus in on those and stop the other ones.

Additional resources: Book: *The New Rational Manager* – Charles H. Kepner.

✪ Tool: Adopting a responsible mindset.

Being a victim gives away your power. This exercise and tool is to enable the inner work to become the best version of you. How you view the world and show up every day is essential to your transformation and success. Your language and mindset play such an important role in your personal success. Are you playing the role of a victim or are you responsible for your actions and what happens to you? A victim frame of mind means you give up your control and feel things happen to you that are beyond your own influence. Whereas a responsible framework means you believe you are an active player in every situation based on your actions. This exercise is adapted from a session I attended with the Trium Group. The purpose of this exercise is to understand how you feel when you are acting victimized as compared to when you take control and are being responsible.

- First pick one of your stories where you feel you were a victim and tell this story for five to 10 minutes to a friend, family member, partner, peer etc. Tell the story with all the emotion of how you felt this other person wronged you. After you have completed your tale, ask the person you just shared this with, on a scale of one to 10 (one low, 10 high), how convincing were you with how you were victimized.

- In your journal or on a piece of paper, write about how you feel. This can be just adjectives, bullets or a paragraph. The essential part is capturing the feelings and the state you are now in.

- It is now time to tell the exact same story for five to 10 minutes to a friend, family member, partner, peer etc., except this time you tell the story where you are fully responsible for the outcome and what happened during this exchange. Yes, this sounds difficult and you are probably thinking how you could have been responsible for what they did to you. Stick with it and tell the story in this new perspective. Same as last time, once you are completed, ask the person you just shared this with, on a scale of one to 10 (one low, 10 high), how convincing were you with how you took responsibility for what had occurred.

- Next to the items you captured after you told the story as a victim, write about how you now feel after taking responsibility.

- Compare the two and reflect and journal on: What wisdom have you just gained from this exercise? How do you feel when you act responsible versus playing the victim? Which one will help you to unlock your full potential? What will you change going forward? Now commit to what you have just decided to do going forward.

Additional resources: Book: *Mindset: The New Psychology of Success* – Carol Dweck.

ⓔ Tool: Emotional Freedom Techniques (EFT) and Matrix Reimprinting.

EFT and Matrix Reimprinting are tools that will help you to address the emotions and beliefs that are tied to your past and you are still living with today. In your life you have developed beliefs, fears and phobias that are holding you back from what you really want. These techniques remove the emotion from the small and big traumas in your past so you can gain the wisdom that the event has to offer you. EFT, which was founded by Gary Craig, is an emotional, needle-free version of acupuncture that works with energy meridians and has been reported in numerous cases to help people overcome emotional, health and performance issues. EFT combines tapping on the energy meridians and using spoken statements to clear energy disruptions or emotional blocks in your body's energy system.

This results in bringing the mind and body back into balance. Matrix Reimprinting created by Karl Dawson, who is one of the 29 EFT Masters worldwide, is a variation on the original EFT protocols, and works with the energy field or matrix that is all around us and is connecting us to our past events. The traumas and stressful experiences in our life are held in the matrix and impact our thoughts, behaviors and actions in the present. As you experience a trauma in your body a part of you splits off or disassociates to the event as a protection mechanism from the trauma event. You may or may not even remember the event after it has taken place. Karl calls these Energy Consciousness Holograms or ECHOs, and Matrix Reimprinting works directly with these ECHOs in the energy field to resolve the negative energy that surrounds them. Both of these techniques provide a way to remove the emotion that is holding you to those events and your past.

In the Desert Storm story I shared in defining your story section in the beginning of this chapter, I did not fully appreciate what I had learned from that day on the battlefield until many years later. Just thinking about that story, which was one of many situations that occurred during my deployment for Desert Storm, was very painful to recall. When I would tell the stories or think about what occurred I would fully relive the event as it was happening back in Iraq. All of the emotions I felt were being experienced again in my body. My heart would start to beat faster, my palms would be wet with sweat and my skin color would go pale. Needless to say, I would bury the memories and pain associated with it. This was status quo until I met an amazing coach, Natasha Abudarham Black, who introduced me to EFT and Matrix Reimprinting. By using these two techniques with me, Natasha helped me to have a major breakthrough of actually realizing I was still reliving post-traumatic stress from being in combat and the emotional toll I was carrying because of it. A common theme throughout this book is awareness and is always the first step to unlocking your real potential for a new result. She helped me to remove the emotions from the event that day in Iraq and to be able to see the wisdom it was meant to give me.

Finding a practitioner and coach who is skilled in these techniques, or attending workshops to develop the skills to work on yourself, will help you to find and release the negative energy and emotions tied to events throughout your life. Each situation where you can remove the emotions allows you to learn new things about those events. The real interesting thing that I experienced is once you start the work on yourself your subconscious begins showing you more and more pictures of moments in your life to gain relief and emotional freedom from. Removing the emotions and not reliving the emotions each day in my life was invigorating and gave me the freedom from them.

Additional resources: Books and website: *Matrix Reimprinting using EFT: Rewrite Your Past, Transform Your Future* – Karl Dawson & Sasha Allenby; *Emotional Freedom Techniques (EFT)* – Gary Craig http://www.eftuniverse.com/ and *The EFT Manual (Everyday EFT: Emotional Freedom Techniques)* – Gary Craig.

Tool: Meditation.

Meditation as a tool helps you to relax, to reduce stress in your life, focus on the present moment to quiet the constant chatter in your mind, and works on the subconscious habits you want to change, while changing your focus to those supportive habits and emotions you want to have in your life. Virginia had a lot of anger in her life and she was having ongoing challenges with cancer of the uterus and had a number of surgeries. When she started meditating using guided meditations from Dr. Joe Dispenza just over three years ago, she was able to change her connection that tied her emotionally to the past emotion of anger and has been cancer free since that time. In her story, meditation became a transformation agent to free her from the anger and she can now use her energy to focus on what she wants in her life. Meditation can be your tool to relax, or in Virginia's situation make a significant change to improve her life. To begin, determine what you want to achieve through meditating and find what works best for you. I have found guided meditations to work best for me and there are a number of options available, I have mentioned a few below in the additional resources.

Additional resources: Books and audio: *Breaking the Habit of Being Yourself: How to Lose Your Mind and Create a New One* – Dr. Joe Dispenza; *Meditation as Medicine: Activate the Power of Your Natural Healing Force* – Dharma Singh Khalsa; *Getting In the Gap* CD – Dr. Wayne W. Dyer; *Wherever You Go, There You Are: Mindfulness meditation for everyday life* – Jon Kabat-Zinn.

Common questions you may have around using tools

When should I use a tool? The above tools give you some options to finding a tool or tools that can work in helping to make the change you are looking for or to become part of your daily success rituals. To help you determine when you should use a tool, becoming aware is essential. The exercises in this book are to help you identify those things you want to work on to transform yourself so you can be the leader you want to be in your life, with your family, community, organization etc. When you find an area you want to work on or you become aware you are in the cycle that you do not want to be in, ask yourself the following questions:

1. Is this a problem I should fix, walk away from or put up with?

2. What tool can help me best with this challenge?

3. Who can I get support from who has already solved this and how did they do it?

4. How can I go within myself and find a solution?

5. What action can I take now to start the momentum to overcome this issue?

Another option is to start by defining what success looks like in one year's time for you in any aspect you want to change. How does it feel, smell, sound like and what do you see? Make the image as vivid as you can with as many details as possible. Also how would you know you have achieved it? What can you do to measure success, how would you feel, and what would people say? With this vision of success, which tools would best help you achieve it? Research, experiment with and choose the ones that resonate most with you and start to build the habit of using them for the next 28 days. What is important is for you to start and build momentum on your action plan immediately. Take action and follow through.

How long do I use a tool? For the tools listed above a number of them are best practices to implement as part of your daily success ritual. For tools like NLP, EFT and Matrix Reimprinting, these also can be used on an ongoing basis. You may find that as you remove the emotion from an event, there will be other aspects to the event that you will uncover and also want to resolve. As a guide always do what feels best to you, and like the 80/20 rule, identify those giving you the best results and use them as long as you feel you are gaining a benefit from them.

How do I know what tool is right for me? It is best to try the ones that resonated with you most first. Have fun and play with them. You want to make this an enjoyable experience and not feel like this is a burden or chore you need or feel compelled to do. The more enjoyable you make it, the more likely you will stick with it, creating the momentum and change you want in your life. The other things that will help you are:

- Find others who have solved what you face and reach out to them. There are a number of support groups you can find that can lend support.

- Build a trusted support group of people with whom you can have open discussions around the tools you are using and get them to share their experience with you.

- Find a practitioner or coach who can teach you more about the tool and help you with mastering the tool.

- Research or use the additional resources I included to understand the tool further. Seek other stories on how people have used them and the results they achieved.

Where can I find resources to help me? The suggestions above of finding a support group, research, reading, audio books, attending seminars, getting a coach are all things I have found to work the best for me. On my journey using these resources, the biggest value was the sensational people I met who were on their own journey. What I have found is when people get together who have the same focus and share their stories, the energy of both people grows and expands. This is such a sensational feeling!

Another resource is to transform your personal device into a learning and motivational platform. You can do this by having audio books, podcasts, meditations, programs and songs that motivate you on it. This way when you have time you instantly have your learning platform available. I use this when I'm training and waiting between appointments to further my knowledge.

Key Points

Your takeaway from this chapter is tools can help you drive your transformation. We covered together:

- Tools can help you drive your transformation and it starts with "what is your story?"

- The power of using tools.

- Tools to use for your transformation, which included: Life Plan and Vision Statement; Vision Boards; Affirmations; 80/20 Rule; Adopting a responsible mindset; Emotional Freedom Technique (EFT) and Matrix Reimprinting; and Meditating.

- Common questions you may have around using the tools.

CHAPTER 4

Success Rituals For A Happy Life

Footprints of past success

Tanya wanted to understand better what most inspired her and the time periods when she was most productive. The reason is she wanted to know what things were fueling her success in order to replicate them. Tanya used self-reflection to look at her career and find patterns where she felt most inspired and productive. She identified three major transitions that resulted in as she explained it "being my best and loving what I was doing moments." As she looked at these different periods she applied the mapping change approach we covered in Chapter 3 (under the 80/20 rule tool section) to determine what made those periods so memorable to her. A common thread was she was at her best when taking on a new assignment, initiative or project, where she did not know a lot about the subject. She enjoyed learning and found by taking the Strengthfinder 2.0 assessment from Gallup that being a learner was one of her top two strengths.

Taking on these new areas and relying on her strength to learn how to do it created energy and enthusiasm for her. This then led to great success in those new activities she was doing. She now understood two of the patterns during the three periods in her life where she was being successful. For her it was a new challenge that she did not know a lot about and the opportunity of using her learning strength to close the gap. What Tanya realized is success leaves footprints for you to find and follow to create even more success in whatever you are doing. Building on what is already strength gave her energy and shifted her view of only working on areas where she had weaknesses. Understanding how well you are doing is the starting point to build success rituals that will create the positive habits that will enable you to succeed with your conscious transformation. In this chapter you will learn to apply success rituals or programs that if you practice and master you will gain the shifts and changes in your life you are looking to accomplish.

To gain an understanding of how aware you are of what success you already have in your life today and what has caused that success to occur, begin by answering the following questions in your journal:

- Looking back at the different aspects of your life to include: school, childhood, sports, community activities, work and others, what are the areas that you feel were successful (experiences that energized you, gave you a feeling of happiness or achievement)?

- For each item you listed what made that experience so special to you?

- What skills or talents were you using and how were you using them or with whom?

- Analyze the list you just created and determine if there are any patterns that are emerging or common themes. Circle or write out the linkages you find.

- Create if-and-then statements to test the patterns you have found within the success events to validate your belief that this combination or single criterion could be the cause or not. From Tanya's story her statement could be: "If the new event is not familiar to me and I am able to learn something new, then I feel energized and excited about the activity." She would then test it against the three periods and would find this to be a relatively true statement. This step provides more clarity.

- Once you have completed the analysis you will have a list of one or many relatively true statements, which like a planning assumption is a fact to be proven or disapproved. How can you test or apply your candidate success criteria to something you are doing today or planning to do to see what difference this will generate?

- Now take action to confirm which items are parts of your footprints to success.

Completing and following through with this exercise identifies important aspects from your past success to formulate and create your success rituals, enabled by identifying something you are already good at and have demonstrated proof. The simplest success ritual and quickest way to success is finding what you do well and doing more of it.

A great way to become aware of what is working well for you is to identify those activities, events or items that make you feel you are doing your best and to track it as you do it. This can be either low to high tech depending on what fits you best. In H. James Wilson's September 2012 Harvard Business Review article titled "You, By the Numbers," he covers the new approach of auto-analytics where you would voluntarily collect and analyze data about yourself to improve choices you make on how you spend your time and apply your energy. The two main types of tools are tracking tools that will help to reveal patterns and "nudgers" that prompt you based on data received or asking you questions. For a low-tech approach you can use a spreadsheet or your journal to capture information about how things like conversations went after you have completed them, what went well, did not go well, the situation etc. For example, I use a simple spreadsheet to track my running activities to determine what is working and what is not. In addition to the basics of date, time and distance, I collect information on the weather, equipment, route and special notes about that training session.

Another example is when I played ice hockey as a goalie. I tracked every game in a notebook. I had the details about the team we played, how the key players moved and like to shoot, the rink, stadium conditions, fans, emotions, my mental state and an analysis of each goal I gave up. This would give me a reference for the next time I played on that team or in that venue, but it also provided my training guide for the next week on where I needed to focus my training. The intent of these tools was to track my performance, make adjustments and understand what worked and did not work for me. Regardless whether you use low- or high-tech tools, the purpose is to help you find what is working and build your steps to success on a strong foundation of your own strengths.

Building the habits that set you up for success

Habits and routines are those non-conscious patterns that are running and driving our behaviors every day. These automatic routines are 95%

of what we do, while only 5% of what we do is conscious. Our habits and routines are either supporting us or they are not. Examples of non-supporting habits are those destructive habits such as smoking, excessive drinking, taking drugs, gambling, self-sabotage or others. Supporting habits would include doing regular physical activity, maintaining a proper diet, proper breathing techniques, drinking enough water each day and others. We create habits by repetition of having the same thought, doing the same action or skill over and over again until it becomes automatic and we do not have to think about the steps required to do it. An example is learning to drive a stick shift car, where at first you were consciously unskilled and needed to maintain focus to do the steps correctly to work the car. As you practiced you became consciously skilled at doing it and from the act of repeating it many times you became unconsciously skilled. This created your new habit of driving a stick shift car.

We can use this same approach to build success rituals. A ritual is consciously developing a routine that will support your transformation or change you want to make. Repeating the routine over and over will make it a habit and just like the learning to drive a stick shift, you will become unconsciously competent at doing it. The essential takeaway is to build the new supportive habit you need to maintain doing the rituals you develop again and again until they form the supportive habit and you do not have to think about. The general rule to form a new habit is you must do the activity daily for at least 28 days straight. If you stop along the way, you will need to restart the 28 days.

Maintaining the activity for 28 days straight is where the challenge will take place. Change can bring discomfort with it and even if the payoff from the change is greater than not changing, people like to do what they are familiar with. How do you maintain the discipline and willpower to sustain doing the same thing over and over enough times to achieve forming the new success habit? In *The Power of Habit* by Charles Duhigg, he covers through showing scientific experiments and stories that willpower is actually a finite resource. Throughout the day your willpower will decrease and depending on the situation it can be used up quicker. He also covers that willpower can be increased and demonstrates ways of achieving this. In one story he highlights how Starbucks teaches new employees routines or procedures to handle stressful situations that could occur in the workplace. This could be a customer not getting the correct order they place or a line forming at the register. By the employee creating and practicing routines to handle the situation with their manager, they were able to deal successfully with the stressful situation without becoming upset. By not becoming upset they were able to maintain their willpower and supported the customer's needs. The idea is by anticipating in advance the event or situation that will cause you to stray from the behavior you want, you can create handling routines and practice them to stay on track with your outcome. This becomes a powerful tool to keep you from not following through with repeating the skill or activity. When Peggy was speaking with me about wanting to start running again, she gave me a list of reasons why she is not doing it today. Using this list, Peggy can build handling routines to set herself up for follow through. One example Peggy mentioned is she prefers to run in the morning, yet she does not want to wake her partner collecting her running kit. The handling routine can be simply to ensuring she takes her running kit that she wants to use from the bedroom the night before and places it where she gets dressed before going for a run. She builds routines that support the habit she wants to create and this starts to remove the excuses.

Another way to build successful habits to support your transformation is to take action and start by taking small steps. Don't overthink it, just do it is the motto to get you into an action state. This can include adding music, do it with a friend, get a coach, make it fun, build on a strength you already have and schedule it. You want to get momentum going in your favor. Willpower is like a muscle that each of us can work on and build it to be stronger.

For my marathon training I will get up at 05:00 when it is raining, snowing or clear skies and run six times a week. My friends will say I'm nuts and then tell me my time I spent in the military gave me the discipline to be able to do my morning runs easily. They believe it is harder for them because they were not in the services and need their sleep. First, this is not true and I normally respond with that is just an excuse or limiting belief holding them back. When I went to running six days a week my inner critic voice was telling me all kinds of things and reasons to stay in bed. I first challenged myself and said to myself, "is this the best excuse that I can come up with?" I would not believe any of what I then would be telling myself. The main thing that gives me the motivation is I know the outcome I want to achieve and my reason why I want that outcome. I set a goal and add a high level of intensity to what it would feel like to achieve my goal. For example, imagining in detail how I will feel when I complete the race and have the medal hanging from my neck. I then create and implement a number of actions that will help me achieve my goal. One of these actions that works for me is I schedule the marathon I will be doing well in advance. I register, pay the entry fees, and book the flights and hotel. Now I have skin in the game and I am committed. The other thing that motivates me to do the training is having already run a marathon. I know if I do not get up and do the training I'm going to suffer on the course and it's going to hurt more when it's done. The intent of my story here is for you to find what motivates and supports you best. Make it happen by taking action.

Taking action

Success can only come by taking action. Being a leader means you are a person of action and this is how you get things done and how your team accomplishes its goals. Actions and thoughts are closely coupled. Your actions come from your thoughts and thus your thoughts are essential to your success. Neural science is showing that thought alone can build neural connections and this becomes a valuable tool for building your success routines. In Dr. Joe Dispenza's book *Breaking the Habit of Being Yourself: How to Lose Your Mind and Create a New One* he demonstrates the value of mental rehearsal and the ability to create new neural networks through the imaging process. His work shows that when a person becomes so involved in imagining the outcome or what they want most in their life, the brain will not know the difference from the imagined or external world. The thoughts themselves are seen as an experience. This means you can create new neural networks by just using your thoughts.

Taking action, repetition and making your daily success routines as automatic as possible is an objective for you to build the habits that set you up for success. This exercise is designed for you to create your daily top 10 to do list and start taking actions to build momentum to make this part of your habits that support you. In this exercise you are to review the tools and techniques that we have covered together in this book and determine which 10 resonate best with you and create your daily top 10 actions you will take. Put these in your journal, schedule them and take action. To assist, here are some example actions to consider as part of your daily action plan:

1. **Journal.** Capture those key things you want to focus on. Writing these down brings more awareness and more awareness will bring more of these essential items into your life. This can include:

   o   What am I grateful for in my life today?

   o   What is really fun in my life?

   o   Where can I add value, where no one else is adding value?

   o   Five things today that I want to achieve before I go to bed?

   o   Before bed, five good things that happened to me today?

   o   Top five successes I had today?

   Every evening I will spend my last hour of the day disconnecting and preparing. I stay away from email, TV, news etc. during this hour. I find if I don't think about these things it positively impacts the quality of my sleep. During this time I will journal about how my day went, what I was grateful for, and acknowledge myself for the things I was really proud of. The secret here is what you capture in your journal is what you get more of in your life. Have an amazing conversation with yourself in your journal every day.

2. **Identify your critical six activities for the day and ensure they are achieved.** These are those amazing things that will move your personal and professional goals forward and are the most important to you. Schedule and do these right away in the morning and any of the items that do not get completed that day, they will become your top actions for tomorrow's critical six activities. This simple action ensures you are achieving the most important things each day and builds your taking action discipline. At the end of the seven-day week you could have achieved 42 activities for your most essential goals you have. In four weeks you then could have achieved 168 actions. This is a major momentum shift for taking action and accomplishing what you want most in your life.

3. **Do your mental work.** I start with my mental review each day with my code of conduct, which covers the areas that are most important to me in my life. My code consists of eight phrases that represent my guiding principles and these are so critical to me that I review them every morning and every evening before I go

to sleep. In addition, in the morning I do what I call my power questions. I mentally review what I am grateful for and ask and answer five power questions. These include a combination of: who do I love, who loves me and how does that make me feel? What am I committed to? What is wonderful in my life? What is fun in my life? What am I excited about in my life? What am I really happy about in my life? What will I do today that makes a difference? How do I need to be to be the person of my dreams? This puts me in a positive mindset, makes me happy and gives me energy. Notice I do not ask myself "why" questions to avoid bringing judgment into this success ritual. I find it very hard to get stressed when I start from a personal high, through asking questions that support me and set me up for success.

4. **Read and listen to inspirational material or music.** I have turned my iPod into my mini learning platform and listen to audio books while I'm stretching in the morning or having breakfast. I then set aside at least 30 minutes in the evening to read inspiring books. I subscribe to motivational speaker Robin Sharma's belief that the books you read and the people you hang out with are who you will be in five years. This is a big idea of set yourself up by listening to and reading material that will empower you to achieve your dreams. The knowledge you gain becomes the working material to support your growth and action plans by giving you new insights into different ways of doing things.

5. **Exercise.** Physical activity makes you feel better, increases your energy and reduces stress. Find an activity you enjoy and build a program that works for you. Be it walking, lifting weights, yoga, calisthenics, riding your bike, swimming, dancing, rowing, running or other activity, take action and commit to do it at least three times a week at the same time to make it a regular part of your routine. Once you feel this is a habit and you are disciplined to stick with it, then increase and add to your program. The most important part is to have fun with it and do it with others, if that works for you.

6. **Affirmation.** An affirmation is a positive thought or phrase, which expresses your desired state you want to achieve. When you repeat, mediate on or visualize them, they become a powerful tool to transform negative beliefs into positive and supportive beliefs.

Create your affirmations and repeat them with energy and passion out loud or to yourself in the morning and evening at least three times each. Reflect in your journal daily your progress and how you are feeling based on your affirmations.

7. **Meditation.** Meditating provides an opportunity to go within and connect with your higher self. It brings calmness, connection, relaxation, joy and many positive benefits. I find using guided mediations work best for me. The ones I enjoy most are from Dr. Joe Dispenza's workshops and CD's that you can purchase from his website, Dr. Wayne W. Dyer "Getting in the Gap" and Kundalini yoga meditation from the audio book, "Meditation As Medicine: Activate the Power of Your Natural Healing Force" by Dharma Singh Khalsa.

8. **Connections.** Being connected with the people we most enjoy being with brings us happiness and when incorporate it into the actions you take. and inspired. Meeting with friends, spending time with your family or helping others with random acts of kindness every day provides you with a purpose of making the world a better place. Building this daily habit brings you greater joy and fulfillment. Your success as a leader depends on people and building a trusting relationship with them. Focusing on how to make your connections stronger, building new ones and actively supporting your connections is an essential daily top 10 action item.

9. **Self-reflection.** "Follow effective action with quiet reflection. From the quiet reflection will come even more effective action", Peter F. Drucker. Take the time to reflect and think. This is an important leadership and conscious transformation tool for your tool kit. Self-reflection gives you confidence, helps get you back on track and in the game if something is not going in the direction you want it to and fuels your growth and development. Use your journal to capture the wisdom you gain from your reflection and incorporate it into your actions you take.

10. **Be in nature.** There is something very peaceful about spending time in nature to connect with your environment and enjoy the moment. Taking time each day to spend time in nature will not only make you feel better, but will give you an opportunity to do

self-reflection. I find adding a daily intention to my time in nature gives me greater purpose for the day. This intention is normally one word of what is important to me that day. Picking up a small stick, leaf, sand or stone and thinking about what I want to leave behind from my life and then placing it back in nature adds power to my time in nature. Play, have fun and find what works for you.

These ten examples provide success rituals that you can incorporate into your daily top 10 actions. A number of these can be combined so you can do them together and not have to over complicate it by thinking "wow, now I have ten more actions on my to do list". For example, while you are spending time in nature you can also journal, do your mental work, self-reflection and your affirmations. In the mornings I will either go for a run or bike ride (exercise) and as I do these activities I do my power questions (mental my metal work) and finish with doing my affirmations. I then stretch, work on my abdominals and weight exercises, while listening to audio books, Podcast or other audio program. This represents the first 60-90 minutes of my day and sets me up to having a stress-free start to my day, being energized and excited about what I'm going to achieve that day. In the evening before going to bed I will meditate, read and write in my journal. This represents another 60–90 minutes and as I disconnect from TV, emails and other distractions, this allows me to sleep extremely well. This became a routine for me and I feel "off" if I miss any part of it.

Why do I work and focus on these success strategies every day? The gift that I was given and the journey this has sent me on continues to be rewarding for me every day. My investment, doing the inner work, being disciplined and following through has given me incredible confidence and courage. I am happier; I'm following my life purpose and my dream daily. This has been the biggest transformation in my life and the results have been great. I received a big promotion in my job, I have a stronger relationship with my loved ones and every day I have a great outlook on life. This was a true game changer. To make your dreams come true each and every one of us must take action and continue to repeatedly follow through until we master the new skill or activity.

Making the Conscious leading journey a possibility

In a classic cartoon you may see the hero making their way through the jungle and all of a sudden they are up to their chest in quicksand with a ferocious alligator ready to pounce and the caption says, "What do you do?" You have a choice and this is what life is all about – the choices that we make. Taking the first step to making your conscious leading journey a possibility only requires you making a choice that you will do it. You are currently standing at the starting point and you have the life that you have created to this point. You have your beliefs, history, and story of how you got to this point, strengths, weaknesses, baggage, relationships, job, physical condition, health, spirituality, energy level, inner voice, habits and knowledge. You may or may not have a vision of where you want to go and you either have a strategy on how to start getting there or not. Perhaps you feel you are missing something in your life; some things are not working the way you want, you feel you have not achieved your life purpose or dreams, you are not fully happy and you want a change. Thinking of having a change in your life brings a sense of excitement, yet it also brings fear and can make you afraid to take that first step. Your inner voice may be telling you to hold off and wait for another day. The step not taken is the one that will be most regretted when your time here is over. "Two roads diverged in a wood, I took the one less traveled by, and that has made all the difference." – Robert Frost. This section is focused on what you can do to take that first step to get you from where you are standing today to start your journey on the road that to date has been less traveled, to achieving your dreams and being extraordinary.

Your vision guides your plan. "Good business leaders create a vision, articulate the vision, passionately own the vision, and relentlessly drive it to completion." – Jack Welch. Organizations can spend hours creating their vision statement and discuss each word multiple times to make sure it sounds just right. I've been in these meetings and when we were done the vision statement sounded good and we had consensus, but we did not necessarily have commitment. Commitment is the key component to take an inspiring vision statement and achieve it with passion. The right vision statement can move a nation like when John F. Kennedy said in his 1961 speech: "I believe that this nation should commit itself to achieving the goal, before this decade is out, of landing a man on the moon and returning him safely to earth." There is a story where President Kennedy was visiting NASA and he asked a janitor what he was doing. The person responded with: "I'm putting a man on the moon." This is what a vision statement with commitment can drive, complete alignment and understanding of how the activities each person takes and does helps to make the vision a reality. This is the same for you working with your team to create your organization's vision or your personal vision statement. Your vision statement is a guide and will change as you learn more. As you are starting out you don't know what you don't know. As you begin learning and experiencing new things on your path, this is where the real transformation takes place in your life. You may adjust your vision statement as you go. To start, capture the essence of where you want to go, you can think of your vision statement as your big dream. It can include anything that feels right to you, not what you think others expect of you, it's your dream. You can use elements of who, what, where and when to create your statement. The how is your strategy and plan to get there. Use motivating language that excites you about your vision. Some examples:

- To live life with passion! Making a positive difference in this world. Being happy and fulfilled. Having an incredible life with my family and friends. Leading by example and setting up brilliant, loving generations to follow.

- Be a fantastic friend to all, making a difference in their lives and being seen as someone who listens, is supportive and truly connected with others and makes them feel outstanding!

- Have financial freedom to support my family and make a significant difference in the world. My destiny is the leaving of an amazing, positive mark on this world, my family and friends. I am moving toward absolute financial freedom, able to make dreams come true!

- Continue to grow my skills and enjoy the process every day of my life. Personal and professional development are two key components of my daily focus areas. This is the juice area that helps me be an exceptional person, leader, manager, coach, spouse, friend and parent.

Use your words and find what works for you. This will become your guiding statement and write it to move you. At least weekly review your statement to keep you on track.

Your code of conduct is your compass. "First say to yourself what you would be, then do what you have to do." – Epictetus. Your code of conduct is your view of what life means to you. It is your principles and values that you follow and honor on a daily basis. This is personal to you and represents how you show up every day and guides how you live. This is a simple list of things that move you and you will capture and review weekly to remind you. I review my code of conduct every morning and evening, because of how important it is to me to live my principles and values. This helps me to be congruent with my actions. I find the following four pillars to be foundational elements to a great life, especially when you can balance and maintain focus on all four. These may give you some ideas to what is important to be part of your compass:

- **Pillar 1: Physical and health.** Being physically fit and taking care of my health by drinking plenty of water and having a proper diet.

- **Pillar 2: Mental (thoughts, clarity, focus).** Being mentally fit with positive focus, observing my thoughts, words and being aware of when my thoughts/words are not supporting me. Your thoughts are very powerful. "Change your thoughts and you change your world." – Norman Vincent Peale.

- **Pillar 3: Emotional (harmony).** Being emotionally fit is realizing the impact your emotions have on your life and cultivating the emotions that give you the highest vibration. In other words, the ones that give you the most energy. Living in the emotions of love, joy and gratitude gives you high energy, whereas being in the emotions of unworthiness, shame, hatred and bitterness gives you low to no energy.

- **Pillar 4: Spirituality (power of being in the moment).** Being spiritually fit is connecting with your higher source, God or other divineness that you have found in your life. I have found this pillar to be the one providing fulfillment in my life that I would not achieve without being in the moment and being connected with my source.

Your code of conduct may include such things as: living honestly; family and friends first; financial security; taking care of the environment; helping others to be successful; making a difference with your actions;

giving back and any other value or principle that is most important to you.

Make your plan a must. This is where your success rituals take over and see you through the difficulties that will pop up to challenge your schedule and commitment to follow through with your action plans. When you look at your schedule for the last week, which six items consumed the most time? Of these six items, which of these were musts that were moving your goals to a better life forward? How many were someone else's musts? Making your conscious transformation action plans a must and being committed is what will drive you to achieve your goals. If you see your transformation journey as a nice to have or should do, you will not follow through when things are difficult and you will remain in the same state you are today. Make your plan a must and schedule it.

Pay yourself first. In George S. Clason's book *The Richest Man in Babylon* he discusses one of the lessons of pay yourself first when it comes to your finances. This concept can be applied to making your conscious leading journey a possibility. First you make your plan a must as covered above and use the critical six actions from the top 10 list in the previous section. Schedule your critical six actions and do these first thing every day. Taking care of yourself is essential to have the life of your dreams. Some people may feel it is selfish to think of themselves first and instead focus only on others. The main idea is as you make the changes and begin to have the shifts you want in your life, you will be able to help even more people. John realized this when he started his conscious transformation journey and ensured he followed through with his action plans. His daily success rituals gave him more confidence and put him at ease. Being in a state of peacefulness and without stress, he was able to listen better to what people were telling him and share how he was able to be calm with his plan he implemented. He was a living example and this is what enabled him to help more people. They saw how he had changed and they wanted the same opportunity. John helped more people by being the change he wanted to see in the world and his actions were the example to reach and help more people.

Minimize and eliminate the zappers. One key element to your happiness is to find out what you love to do and direct all your energy toward doing it. Either minimize or eliminate all the other things that zap your energy and take your time away from what you love to do. The first step is to find what you love to do. Make a list of all the things you enjoy. Next to each item write the last date you actually did that activity. Now it is time to find and eliminate your energy zappers. What things are you doing to just occupy your time and are not moving your life goals forward? These are things that drain you or are just fillers. Your list may include TV, food, people, and parts of your job, events, news, internet or others. Next to each item that you have listed, record how much time you spend on that activity per day and week. This will help you to become aware of how much time goes toward or is used up by these activities. Make a commitment and plan to reduce these items. Keep reducing the time spent on the ones you want to change until you feel you have achieved what you want to accomplish. Use the extra time you have gained back into your schedule and make a commitment to do the things you captured that you love to do and schedule them into your calendar.

Be a master of your inner critic. Your inner critic can be harsh and demanding. The biggest obstacle you will face is overcoming your fear and the critic who will say you are not doing it right, this is too difficult, and you can always start tomorrow. This critic will remind you and show you that you lack the faith in yourself to follow through with your program. Your inner critic may have listened to all the negative comments that have left their wounds on you from the past. Your grade school teacher, a friend, family member or someone else who said you were not good enough. Becoming aware is an important step to master your inner critic. Carrie recently went to a conference with her new client and the topic of the meetings was about a part of the business she did not believe she has mastered yet. Carrie's inner critic was telling her she was not good enough, she was dumb, unattractive and when the inner script starts playing it brings everything up, not just about the topic at hand. As she was in this victim mindset, she saw evidence from the environment to back up her critic. At dinner no one spoke with her and she said to herself, see no one likes you because you are so… fill in the blank. On the bus ride back to the hotel, she experienced the same thing. No one sat next to her and the scripts started all over again. The next day however she was in a better mood and all of a sudden people were engaging and speaking with her. Carrie realized she had just been handed a gift. The first day her victim mindset was sending out a vibration that others picked up on subconsciously and they avoided her. The next day her vibration was positive and this attracted people to her. This awareness is essential to see the impact her critic and mindset was causing. With the awareness, she is working on mastering her critic by being positive, doing affirmations and cutting the emotional connections to the past events with tools we have covered in this book together like EFT and meditation. She is demonstrating her courage to let it go. She is playing more and having fun. These will help her to quiet the critic and be more successful and happy with her life.

How do you know you are getting there and you are making progress on your journey? As you journal and do your self-reflection you will begin to notice shifts in your life. Some may come very quickly and some may build on others. You will notice you feel different. Things in your environment that used to cause you to react do not have the same impact on you. You may realize internal shifts that all is within you and you have the ability to change. As you begin to change the world starts to change around you. You will see, feel, sense or hear a difference and you will then know you are well on your way to the life you have always wanted.

Key Points

Your takeaway from this chapter is how to build success rituals to support you having a happy life. We covered together:

- Success leaves footprints and you can replicate them for greater success in your life.

- Habits represent 95% of what we do on a daily basis and how you can use habits to support your goals to achieve what you really want.

- What defines your success is the type of actions you take. Building your top 10 daily actions and making them a habit will fuel the change you want to have in your life.

- A big factor in your success is just taking that first step. This can be accomplished by creating your vision, capturing your code of conduct to be your life compass, making your plan a must do for you, paying yourself first and scheduling the important things you want to achieve daily, eliminating the energy zappers, and becoming a master of your inner critic. No need to be a harsh judge of yourself, instead be supportive with love, encouragement and kindness.

PART II

Being A Leader of Your Transformation And Making A Difference For Others

CHAPTER 5

Everyone Is A Leader

Everyone can be a leader

A number of people believe that to be a leader they must have a title that demonstrates they are a leader. Some will argue leaders are born and some that leaders are developed. In addition to looking at titles and position in the hierarchy, people look at the big names and say, "Yes they are a leader because I always read about them or see their names associated with being a leader in their industry, company, community, church, and schools." There are countless theories on how to become the best leader you can be. I have been trained through the U.S. military to be a leader and the U.S. military has some of the best schools to develop your leadership capabilities. The U.S. Army Ranger School is the best example I have experienced on building your leadership skills and understanding your potential.

While less straightforward to understand the path forward to advancing your leadership skill as the military, the corporate world has numerous programs to develop and create leaders. What I have experienced is leadership really comes down to your belief and mindset about being a leader. All of the training programs and experience will give you more opportunities to learn and acquire knowledge and these will make you better at doing your job or task; however they will not make you a leader unless you feel you are a leader. You are a leader in everything you do; you just may not believe it yet.

Hanna is a recently promoted manager and by her title you can say she is a leader. Hanna's mindset has not shifted to where she believes she is a leader yet. The training sessions, mentoring and feedback in leadership talent reviews highlights she is gaining the knowledge, but is not applying it from feeling, being and acting as if she believes she is a leader. The shift that must occur is she has to feel and believe she is a leader. Once she makes the change, the knowledge she is gaining will be applied from her being a leader and the wisdom she then gains from being in this mental framework will show up in everything she does. She will be a leader.

The concept of being a leader is all about a shift in perception that you are a leader and applies to every aspect of your life. A leader is not someone who always has to be leading from the front, giving commands, handing out work assignments, or be in the spotlight. In Ranger school we would refer to the people who would only act as a leader when someone was watching as a spotlight ranger. A leader is everyone and in everything they do as long as they believe it. A parent who reads a story to their child or children at a school event is being a leader. A person who is working multiple jobs to provide their family a place to live and food to eat is being a leader for their family. A teacher helping their students to learn new things is being a leader. A sales clerk helping a customer identify what paint they need for their home improvement project is being a leader at that given point in time. Being a member of a sports team and playing your position the best you can and helping your other teammates is being a leader. A key component that makes this leading is they are setting an example in everything they do or don't do. That setting an example is leading. People step up and provide examples every day. A random act of kindness of helping someone in need or just to help them is setting an example and being a leader. You are a leader in everything you do.

The shift in your perception that you are a leader is your opportunity to embrace this concept and live your life as a leader of your conscious transformation, becoming the person you want to be, making a difference in your life and the world and becoming a conscious leader. The benefit is you are taking charge and being accountable for the results that you are getting in your life and if the results do not match what you want, lead yourself in changing them. When you adopt this empowering mindset you start to ask yourself empowering questions like I am a leader at this, how can I be the best at doing it? What would the best person in the world at doing this be doing? This empowering shift begins to build greater confidence and courage to do even more leading in other aspects of your life. This chapter is about you being a leader to lead your personal transformation, your team, and organization or just being a better version of you each day. It starts with you believing you are a leader and you are a leader in everything you do each day, because everything you do is an example in one way or another.

Being a leader is about what you do

Being a leader all starts with you and your view on being a leader. Can you believe and develop the belief that you are a leader in everything you do today? Take a few moments to capture in your journal the answers to the questions below. The purpose of this exercise is to provide you with awareness on how you perceive leadership, if you feel you are being a leader today or not and to give insight to what could be preventing you from being a leader today. With awareness you can make different choices and this will lead to different results.

- What does leadership mean to you?

- What does being a leader mean to you?

- Where are you being a leader today in your life?

- Where are you not being a leader today?

- What is the reason you feel you are not being a leader in this area above?

- If you are not being a leader today in your life, where could you be a leader?

- What would it take for you to feel you are a leader?

- What is preventing you today from being a leader?

- What else is preventing you from being a leader today?

From completing the above awareness exercise, you will now have an understanding of your current belief on being a leader. Belief is the critical shift to get you on your way to being a leader. To build on reinforcing your view that you are already a leader or to start the process of taking on this persona of being a leader, start by assuming you are a leader today and act as a leader. I'm not talking about faking it until you make it. If that works for you then feel free to do it. I'm getting you to focus on claiming your role and position as being an example in everything you do and get you to begin behaving as a leader. Your focus here is to start looking at how you can be the best and do the best you can at what you are doing. This change in your focus will drive your energy into this space, expand your awareness and get you to start asking yourself questions that empower you to act more as a leader. These will be questions such as: How do I need to feel to be a leader in what I'm doing? What does a leader doing this do to set a great example? How do I need to be to be a leader at what I do? What do I need to know? What do I need to do? These questions are the framework of the Be, Know, Do model that you will use as one of your guiding principles to being a leader.

The Be, Know, Do model comes from the U.S. Army Leadership Field Manual. The three components from the manual cover:

- Be – this covers your character as a leader which is essential to you leading. Your character gives you the courage to do what is right without regards to the circumstance or consequences. Another component is being aware of your core personal values.

- Know – the knowledge and skill sets to be a leader, which are covered in four areas: Interpersonal, Conceptual, Technical and Tactical skills. Mastery in these is essential to success.

- Do – leaders take action and bring together everything they are, believe, know to give purpose, direction and motivation to their organization. The three leader actions: Influencing, Operating and Improving.

The Be, Know, Do framework gives you the components to personalize the three elements to your platform of being a leader. You can do this as one overall model representing how you want to be a leader in your life and/or you can use it for each area in your life you are being a leader in. This could be doing one for being a leader at work, being a leader with your family, being a leader with your community and the other areas of your life. The purpose of creating these is to:

- Keep you focused on what you what to be, while leading in these areas.

- Guide you in your knowledge capture plan, development and how you will proceed toward mastery.

- Create action focus by driving you to take action based on putting all three elements together.

- Provide a map and plan to being the leader you want to be.

To build your **Be, Know, Do** framework for your overall model or for each area in your life you will be leading in, complete the following exercise.

1. Name your **Be, Know, Do** model at the top of your page.

2. On your paper write the three components **BE, KNOW, DO** and give yourself space next to each to capture notes from the next action steps.

3. Next to **DO**, write down what values and attributes will shape your character leading in this area. Look at these as internal and qualities that you possess at all times. What are those things that make up your identity as being a leader? What are your values? These can also be aspirational by thinking about a leader you know or have read about, and what qualities have made them a great leader in doing what they do or in this area.

4. Next to **KNOW**, write down these four skills and give yourself space to write next to them:

   o Interpersonal skills: any skill you use for interacting and communicating with and getting along with others.

   o Conceptual skills: includes such things as creative thinking, analyzing, and understanding complicated or abstract ideas.

   o Technical skills: skills that are specific to a certain job or career.

o Tactical skills: skills that can give you an advantage like using your past experience, success rituals etc.

Next to each one capture what knowledge and skill sets you believe you need to have to master this area of being a leader.

5. For each knowledge and skill set you have written down, determine which are strength areas already for you today. Where are you already a master? In what areas will you need to develop and acquire more training, knowledge and skill? This will assist you later in building your development plan.

6. Next to DO, what actions do you need to do on a short-term, mid-term and long-term basis to lead in this area? As you review the action list, categorize these actions also as to whether: they are a one-off action or an ongoing action item. If they are an ongoing action item, are they done daily, weekly, monthly or yearly?

Part of being a leader is to know your strengths and opportunities for development. The above exercise will help you to understand your strengths and opportunities. To help you further, the two exercises below will give you more insight. To be a leader, you need to understand your starting point of what works for you today and what does not. This will help you to build out your development plan to become the leader you want to be in every aspect of your life.

✒ Exercise: Getting to knowing yourself better

1. In your journal, conduct your personal Intellectual Property (IP) inventory by writing down all those things you feel make you special and add value to your job, family, community and any other aspect of your life.
2. What things do others compliment you on or highlight as your strengths?
3. What are you known for? If you find this challenging to complete by yourself, then try the exercise of contacting 10 people to give you feedback.

Examples could include: Gets things done; gets the best out of people; knows how to make the best cakes; dedication; always has a smile and sees the best in everything.

🌀 Exercise: Finding your strengths and opportunities

1. On a piece of paper, spreadsheet or in your journal make two columns. Name one of the columns "things that I enjoy" and the other column "things that I do not enjoy."

2. Take your time and under each column list those things you do daily, weekly, monthly or yearly that either give you joy or don't. If you enjoy an activity, you get lost in time when you do it and feel great about it, this is an item for your enjoy list. If you dread the activity, keep putting it off, this is an item for your do not enjoy list.

3. Once you have completed the two lists, look at each column and analyze the items you have listed. Are you seeing any common themes appearing in each of the two columns? Identify your common themes and group them together. Do you have a title for those groupings? If yes, add a title to them.

Being a leader is an ongoing focus and work to refine and build your skills toward mastery. The exercises you have completed so far will give you a good starting point for building out your leadership plan.

Demonstrating your leadership

Now you have shifted your belief to you are now a leader in everything you do and you have a framework to develop your leadership skills, where can you demonstrate being a leader? Start by leading yourself. To break away from being ordinary, the 75% to 80% of leaders who have made no lasting impression and are forgettable, it starts with the decision that you want this to be a must in your life. Make the firm decision that you are a leader and then you begin your transformation journey. The change you want to have in your life comes from within you. Hoping the world changes without you changing from the inside will lead to you getting and having the same life tomorrow and the day beyond as you have today. Then you will stay the same and not have the life of your dreams. It all starts with you and being the example of change and setting the example in everything you do.

The places you can demonstrate being a leader is in every aspect of your life. The big idea is to look actively for opportunities in your environment and life to take action and do something positively different to begin your change. The more and more actions you take and the more results you see from those actions, the more momentum builds toward being the leader you want to be. As the momentum grows you will become more moved by the experience and this leads to even greater successes along your conscious transformation path. These successes and feelings associated with the experience will lead you to want to repeat the process and do more to fuel your growth. Your journey begins to pick up speed and the learnings you gain grow exponentially with it. The following categories represent aspects that could be in your life and a few suggestions of how to begin being a leader in these areas to start building your successes and gain momentum with your transformational journey. These areas when in alignment with how you want to be and show up also build your energy as we discussed in Chapter 1.

Being a leader in your home. The home environment provides a great opportunity to demonstrate leadership with simple random acts of kindness to others in your household and setting an example for others in your home. The home also creates a challenge as everyone in the environment knows each other's habits extremely well. Each family member plays a role they tend to be emotionally attached to and they may not react favorably to changes you are making in your life. Each member also knows the emotional weapons to deploy on each other to get the other to react the way they expect. These weapons can be shame, guilt or many others. These are deployed unconsciously and are very effective when they are used. You can expect to see these as the changes you are making can challenge the others and they may begin to question themselves. They can even put pressure on you to go back to the way you were. This is a key obstacle you will face early in your journey. Being aware of the emotional weapons that work on you and being able to handle this influence from your family to continue your transformation is the key to your success or failure. My experience is that as long as you remain committed to your internal changes, do not worry about what others think, and elicit their active support in helping you, you will make it through any opposition that could come up. A simple but effective mantra is, "I say yes to my conscious transformation and say no to feeling guilty about it and worrying what others say or think about me." The magic is as you stay committed to change, the world begins to change. Some actions you can do to start leading in the house:

- Step up and start doing something different. If you typically do not do certain chores in the house, take action and start doing them.

- If you always talked about something you wanted to do in or outside the house to improve it, take action to complete it.

- Set an example by turning off the TV and having a discussion with the family on a topic of interest.

- Be an example by doing exercise and following healthy nutrition.

- Try new things together. You can create an ideas or to do jar and put pieces of paper with different activities on them in the jar. You can schedule a day or more in the month when you will select an idea from the jar and do the activity on the piece of paper.

- Read a story to your children and poetry to your partner.

Being a leader at work. The work environment provides numerous chances to be a leader. Every action you take or don't take has an impact on you, your customers, team, organization and company. You are either making a difference or blending in by being average. Stepping up and showing up to be the best in everything you do builds energy and gives you the feeling of knowing you have done your best each day. This feeling makes your work life more personally rewarding and this has a trickle effect impact of improving the other areas in your life. Make the decision to be the best and do the best you can at everything you do. Be the example of your own excellence. Here are some suggestions of things you can do in the work environment to be more of a leader:

- Master what you do and continually drive your own development in both your strengths and weaknesses. Others can help, but you own your development plan.

- Every interaction with a customer is an opportunity to connect and make them feel special. Be the person making them feel special, even when they are not happy.

- Offer help to a teammate, another group or someone just in need, with no expectations of getting something in return.

- Act as a leader by participating and speaking up with your thoughts on how to make things better.

- Be a team player, share your knowledge and help your team be a better team.

- Volunteer for assignments, tasks and jobs.

- Mentor and or train someone.

- Commit to having deeper relationships and have discussions that are enriching to others and you. Get beyond the coffee side chitchat to meaningful dialog on things that are inspiring and uplifting.

Being a leader in your community, club, team or other. Your community, club, team or other group you belong to gives you an opportunity daily to demonstrate your leadership by being a positive example. These are some ideas to start demonstrating your leadership within your own community environment:

- Vote – this not only sets an example, but also is your individual act to participate in the process to select the leadership that represents what you want to see in your community.

- Volunteer and help out – give back to those in need, to just make a difference or be a part of something bigger.

- Be of service – helping your neighbor, local school, sporting team or just picking up trash on the ground. Be a difference with your actions.

- Activism – lead, speak up or be part of a movement for a change for your community that will make a positive difference for all those who live there.

- Be a great follower – following well is leading by doing your part to make the whole better. Be supportive and help the leaders implement the ideas that make a positive difference for the entire group.

These lists represent a few actions you can take to begin demonstrating being a leader. Your opportunity is to add to the list and create your own list for the different aspects in your life. Next is to pick the ones that resonate with you and start taking action. Action leads to results and results lead to momentum to fuel your conscious transformation to live the life you want to live.

Building a leader mindset and being a leader

Taking action is a method to demonstrate being a leader. Constantly building a leadership mindset is essential to being a successful leader in everything you do. Taking action can only do so much for you if you do not believe you are a leader. You begin building a leader mindset by defining what leadership means to you and then living it each day in your life. Let's look at a couple of definitions to see what common elements can be used to help defining what leadership can mean to you. Motivational speaker and author of *The Leader Who Had No Title*, Robin Sharma's quote: "Leadership is about having unshakable faith in your vision and unrelenting confidence in your power to make positive change happen," focuses on your faith and confidence to make change happen. U.S. Army Manual FM 6–22 definition: "Leadership is the process of influencing people by providing purpose, direction, and motivation while operating to accomplish the mission and improving the organization." The manual further states: "An army leader is anyone who by virtue of assumed role or assigned responsibility inspires and influences people to accomplish organizational goals. Army leaders motivate people both inside and outside the chain of command to pursue actions, focus thinking, and shape decisions for the greater good of the organization." These two military examples highlight influencing, motivating and making a difference for the best of the organization.

Now in your journal write down what you believe leadership is to you. With this definition, what characteristics, behaviors and actions do you feel are critical to become and demonstrate every day in your life to be an example of the definition that you created? How would you need to act and what do you need to feel to live like this daily? How would you need to be to achieve this? These items you just captured in your journal is your blueprint to building the leader mindset and being the leader you want to be. Next, you start living these each day by setting your intention and focusing on being this leader.

As you strengthen your leadership mindset that you are focusing on, being a leader has other components that make leading exciting and can take you to another level in your development and transformation. The first element is about speaking your truth. This is being compassionate, caring for others and saying what is in your heart. Fear is an emotion that keeps people playing small and wanting to be safe. Being afraid to speak up and just being quiet will make you another non-memorable leader in what you do. Your leader mindset is about speaking your truth, and as Dr.

Seuss states, "Be who you are and say what you feel because those who mind don't matter and those who matter don't mind." The second area is trust your instincts. You will never have all the information or data to make a decision. Build your leader mindset with trusting your gut feeling about the situation. Build your intuition by focusing on it and journaling. Each day capture those intuitive moments you had and what the results were from it. Doing this exercise will strengthen your mindset by showing you examples of where you are already being more intuitive each day in your life. The third area is all about putting other people first. If you want to be a leader in a team environment it is essential you put your team and people before yourself. I have interviewed a number of people who have wanted to be managers and when you ask them why they want to be a manager, it would surprise you how many never mention people at all in their response. In your leadership mindset, it's essential that people are a key focus. This is the essence of leading in every area of your life, making a difference for others. The fourth area of being a leader is what I call the essential three resources and how you use them. As a leader, how you use your time, what you focus on and your personal energy are the three things you bring to everything in your life. Your leader mindset is all about being aware of how you are using these essential three resources and how you want to use them for the greater good of what you want to achieve. These four elements when combined to become part of your leader mindset will help you to develop your leadership skills further and the result is you will begin to see you are living like the leader you want to be.

What makes a leader today?

Being a leader today is having a willingness to be one and being committed to doing it right. It includes what we have covered so far in this chapter. It is having the belief you are a leader in everything you do, building your plan, creating your definition and having the mindset to live up to your definition. Being a leader is putting this all together and developing yourself and driving toward being a master. For becoming the conscious leader you want to achieve this is the development and focus model we will use:

Master your leadership: This part of your ongoing focus and development plan will all be about those things that relate to you becoming a leader and mastering it. Here you will take the answers to the questions that you completed as part of your awareness exercise on:

- How do you perceive leadership?

- Do you feel you are being a leader today or not?

These will give you insight to what could be preventing you from being a leader today. Based on what you have captured, prioritize the items and select the top three you will focus on during the next 12 months. From the Tools That Drive Your Transformation chapter, either add these three priorities to your life plan or use the methodology highlighted in that tool to build your plan on how you will work on these three elements.

Master your craft: Your craft is your job, life calling, passion, art or things you do or want to do. For this part of your focus and development plan use the items from the KNOW and DO section of the model you created in the Be, Know, Do exercise to create your development plan. As above, prioritize and pick the top three items you want to work on during the next 12 months or sooner. Use the same methodology to build out what you want to achieve, your reason to do it and goals that will help you achieve them.

Master yourself: Doing the inner work is the most essential component for being a conscious leader. Based on what we covered and the exercises you completed in the first three chapters, what are the top three items you want to focus on and develop over the next 12 months or sooner? Again create goals to help you achieve them.

This model will keep you focused on the essential three elements of: master your leadership, master your craft and master yourself. Having three top priorities for each that you are working on to develop further is the foundation for your development mastery plan.

Being a leader today is also about striving for the next level of excellence in what you do. It is part of the secret sauce that goes with your mastering of the above areas. It is the part that distinguishes you and best elevates your skills in order to become one of the 20–25% of those memorable leaders. A number of organizations and companies will look outside their team to find the next leader or person to fill a key position. Part of this is the people within the group are known and are not demonstrating the leadership in what they do, as we have been discussing. Another reason is the people within a group tend to be really focused on what I call their coconut and miss the tree or entire jungle. What organizations want and need is people who are leading in what they do and are outstanding at this formula: I (innovative thinking) + T (thought provoking) + PR (proven results) = HP (high potential). If you are leading and focusing only on your coconut, you are not seen as a high potential and will stay doing what you are doing unless you leave or are let go. This formula highlights it is about your ideas, speaking your truth, having a track record of achieving results. It takes all three components to go to the next level. If you are seen as a dreamer and cannot deliver the results, you will not be seen as the full package. Likewise if you are just seen as an executer, same applies. The enabling factor is you have the ability to present and communicate the concept and ideas. The takeaway is these are the elements that when combined with your development plan and focus on being a leader, you will be reaching that higher plane that most people will never reach. This is the next climb up on the mountain of your change. Being a leader today is more than the willingness to be one and being committed; it includes the daily focus, development, activities and success routines to drive and achieve your plan of being the leader you want to be.

Key Points

Your takeaway from this chapter is that you are a leader in everything you do. We covered together:

- Being a leader is about your shift in perception, your belief that you are a leader.

- Being a leader is about what you do. We covered the Be, Know, Do framework and how to use it in your leadership transformation.

- Demonstrating your leadership is everything you do and your environment. We looked at actions you can take to build your momentum in leading at home, work, and your community, club, team and other groups.

- The elements of building a leader mindset by defining what leadership is to you and living this every day of your life.

- We covered what makes a leader today and the framework of your development by focusing on mastering your leadership, mastering your craft and mastering yourself.

- We looked at the formula: I (innovative thinking) + T (thought provoking) + PR (proven results) = HP (high potential) as a way of taking your leadership to an even higher level and further distinguishing yourself.

CHAPTER 6

The New Domain Of Leadership

Old school leadership is no longer the rule

The conference room was full with all of the organization's leadership waiting for the senior leader to come in and give an update to the team before heading out to an organized fun event including the entire 200 plus people. The senior leader entered the room and began by saying, "You've all let me down and are not doing your job. You are all a failure. Our top measurement of customer satisfaction is the lowest compared to the other teams in our larger organizations and this is unacceptable. If I'm going to go down I will take every one of you with me. I expect you to turn it around immediately and there will be no vacation or business travel until this is fixed." The leader then left the room. The tension and atmosphere was intense and you could see the shock and dismay on the leaders' faces within the room. This true-life example plays itself out more often than you would expect. You may have many other stories that are similar or worse. This is an example of not winning the hearts and minds of the people you are entrusted to lead. Coercion, threats and relying on punishment as a motivator is an old school leadership methodology of punishing the masses for any perceived fault and expecting peer pressure will take care of the rest. The leader can just sit back and everything will fall into place. This is an organizational practice that resembles the old military discipline practice of a blanket party, where the drill sergeant makes the entire platoon do physical labor because one person made a mistake. The intent is the others will enforce the discipline on the outcast by giving them a blanket party to conform to what everyone else is doing. This would mean a group of soldiers, normally sometime in the night while the targeted one was sleeping, would sneak up to their bunk, hold a blanket over them while others would hit or punch the recipient. It is an outdated form of motivating and when used within an organization causes resentment and distrust for the leader.

Vasos wanted to get feedback from his manager on how he was performing and what he should be focused on for the upcoming fiscal year. His leader fit a standard mode in this organization, where the best subject matter expert, someone who was really good at being a client consultant would then be selected to be the manager of the team. The manager was great at being a consultant and continued to do this while he was the leader of the team. This continued to earn him praise and respect from his leadership, while his employees were left on their own to figure out how they were doing or what they should be doing in the future. This is a classic example, because the team was performing based on the numbers. To get his performance review from his manager, Vasos had to take the subway in London in the opposite direction from his home to ride with his manager in the direction to his home. Going out of his own way was the only chance Vasos had to get any feedback or meeting from his leader. Vasos left the company shortly after that and was hired by a company who respected him and where he is now thriving. The saying is around 80% of the people who leave a company do so based on their manager and my experience shows this to be very accurate. Keeping your employees in the dark, not having open and inspiring two-way performance conversations is an old school leadership methodology to giving no meaningful feedback. A leader using this methodology believes in feedback only if something is wrong. No news is good news.

In a cost-savings move the company decided to remove the healthy free fruit that was available for the employees for snacking during the day. In lieu of the fruit, the company installed vending machines with sugar snacks of candy and chips that the employee could purchase. This move made financial sense to the leadership. Adding the vending machines was a no-thought decision. Rather than thinking about the long-term impacts that these sugar snacks and chips would have on the employees' health, the future cost of absenteeism from health issues that could arise or potential increasing medical insurance cost, a short-term financial decision was made with no thought to the long-term impact this could have on the employees. Making short-term financial decisions without regard to the impact on your people is an old school leadership methodology of increase profits and cut cost is all the company is about, everything else comes after.

Charlie did not want to share his knowledge with the team and would not train anyone else to know how to make the system changes needed to support the organization. Charlie believed that by keeping the knowledge to himself, he was making himself indispensable and protecting his job. Charlie was very knowledgeable in what he did, but he was not a team player and the other team members did not trust him. Charlie's career stalled until he realized through the feedback his leader provided that he needed to act as a leader within the team and share and train his peers. Thinking about your own interest and not supporting your team members and helping them to be better is an old school personal leadership methodology of putting yourself ahead of others to distinguish yourself as the go to person because of your special knowledge. Once Charlie gave up this belief and changed, he was able to take on new things, which led him to be promoted a year later.

These four examples demonstrate traits that are part of what I call the Stone Age of leadership. A period in time that is extinct to the way people want to be led today. The challenge is these dinosaur ways of leading are still pervasive in workplaces today and are causing great talent to be ordinary at best or leave to join other organizations. The cost to employee morale, productivity, turnover cost and the overall impact to the organization these leaders cause can be staggering. Another challenge that I have seen in my 30 years of experience is this cost or impact is rarely tracked. If the leader is delivering on their primary responsibilities of the sales number, critical Key Performance Indicators (KPI), successfully achieving their missions or managing up well to their superiors, how they are doing it does not matter. As long as the leader does not do something ethically or morally wrong, they tend to remain in position causing more damage. These leaders are the ones who fill the ranks of those leaders we never want to work for again.

The next group of forgettable leaders that make up the 75% to 80% of leaders most people do not want to work for again are the ones who are average in what they do. They may be good administrators, get along well with people or get the job done. You may have even liked them. They just didn't move or inspire you to be more. These leaders normally have not had a good example to follow to show them a different way of doing things. I find a lot of new leaders are not very good at giving employees feedback, coaching them, building development plans or giving performance reviews. When I ask them about how they learned their skills, the answer is always, "This is how my leaders did it with me." The cycle ends up feeding itself and we end up with more and more leaders being the same. These leaders end up continuing to lead in an average way, which impacts the people they are entrusted to lead. The same results are achieved and another group of employees are asking themselves is this as good as it gets?

The answer is learning from the 20–25% of those leaders who have inspired us and moved us to want to work with them again. We learn by looking at the traits they demonstrate every day and emulating them to be part of our life. Leading in the conscious way is taking consistent actions that make a positive difference for your people, family, friends, community, organizations, and environment, while making the world a better place to live. A conscious leader is everyone who makes the decision to be one, believes in their heart they are a leader and takes the steps to live and be an example for the world to follow. Imagine what your home, work and community environment would be like if everyone would embrace conscious leading. This is how we change the world together and begin to make the changes required to make the world a better place. The benefits are we all enjoy more happiness in every aspect of our life, which leads to less stress and a healthier lifestyle. We are able to enjoy the journey and the things we do. It all starts with embracing the new domain of leading, which is be conscious and focus your energy on making a positive difference in everything you do.

Doing both by being in the game and enjoying playing

Conscious leading scares some leaders when they hear about it and they associate it with being a new buzzword or part of the New Age movement, which means someone who combines Eastern and Western spiritualism along with self-help, motivational psychology, quantum physics and holistic health. These leaders feel being a conscious leader means they must fully embrace the spiritual route of enlightenment, while others believe they only need to attend training on emotional intelligence to be able to control their own emotions. The leader who wants to focus on being a conscious leader asks questions like what about pursuing my goals, wanting to achieve higher levels in the organization and have material possessions in my life? Conscious leading is taking positive actions to make a difference for others and themselves. It is about giving to others and graciously receiving. It is about being an example for others, your mindset, your actions, and where you focus and place your energy. You can do both, enjoy the journey of your transformation, by taking the time to experience what you learn, while you also pursue your goals, achievements and personal possessions.

Melissa Rancourt is an example of a leader who does both well. Melissa is the owner and managing director for Greenlight Project Management, founder and chair for Greenlight for Girls Foundation, owner of Serendipity Wellness Spa, owner of Serendipity Spa brands and head of faculty for Boston University Brussels. She has embraced conscious leading while blending her spirituality and being focused on achieving her goals. The two aspects have actually become an integral part of who she is and there is no real separation of the two. They just go naturally together as this is highlighted when Melissa states, "I am often traveling to various countries and juggle 10–15 projects at one time. My favorite moments are when I can convince a CEO to embark on a community project with the sole intent to help others, to show teams that work can be fun and not so serious and to celebrate accomplishments with laughter and the feeling of fulfillment." The goal, achievement and being all become one and this is how conscious leaders can do both.

To Melissa conscious leadership means, "Leading in a conscious way is harnessing your energy to stay strong and to help others. Conscious leadership is using all of your life experiences to make conscious decisions on your own future and the future of those you impact. Conscious leadership is igniting the passion in those around you and engaging others to lead and to follow. Conscious leadership is the understanding that life is bigger than one individual, bigger than just you. Conscious leadership is being in the moment, consciously being in the present, taking in your surroundings and making good, solid decisions that better the lives of others. Conscious leadership can also be about dealing with risk, uncertainty and challenges that will arise professionally and personally." How is she able to do both and be a conscious leader? It is how she manages her energy and her beliefs. For replenishing her energy, she says, "The work that I do makes me happy, helping others and making a difference – this gives me energy. Volunteering in our non-profit is my personal reward for working long hours. Every day, I give my personal time to encouraging societal work – whether in our NGO or another community effort – sometimes I can only give one hour a day and sometimes 10 hours in a day – each moment is fulfilling and fills me with energy to accomplish anything I set my mind to." And her beliefs: "I believe that anything is possible. I believe in seeing the positive in any situation. I believe that life is short and we are here to make a difference in the world. I believe that our lives, personal and professional, are full of serendipitous moments that can create the paths we take – if we are ready to see and take action. These beliefs help me to manage balancing my personal energy, spiritual connection and conscious leading."

Melissa's story demonstrates you can do both well and you can sense the fun she is having when you meet and speak with her. Her energy is infectious. Having fun as you are doing anything makes it easier and enjoyable. Her advice to people who are becoming a conscious leader: "A conscious leader uses their beliefs and philosophy in life to guide them in making decisions that better the world around them. Reflect on what you believe in and what you are here to accomplish. Feel confident in your path and set your own destiny." With this advice a critical component to being a conscious leader is taking the steps to change and transform from where you are today to where you want to go. Transformation is about achieving a noticeable change for the better in your life. This can equal being less stressed, more confident, engaging in discussions with all your connections, better awareness, having higher energy levels, new ways of looking at things and many more. As you begin your path to transforming to how you want to be, together we will cover a number of methods and tools in this book to guide you like a traveller using a compass. Thus the best way to enjoy your journey is to have fun with it. See the world from the wonder of being a child, when they are free and are at play. I call this "kinder herz," experiencing every day with a child's heart. One favorite school activity children like to do is go on field trips to see and learn about new things. Approach your change as an adult field trip and learn from the wisdom you will gain. Play and learning are interconnected as Fred (Mr) Rodgers' quote highlights: "Play is often talked about as if it were a relief from learning. But for children play is serious learning. Play is really the work of childhood." Having fun will enhance your learning process as you are making the changes to improve your life.

The new way of leading others

The old school way of leading within the world is not achieving the results we are looking for. We are witnessing social and political models that are no longer working. Economies are struggling and the future is uncertain for many people. Sustainable solutions are required to make changes and we need a new way to do it, as Albert Einstein so accurately states: "The world's problems cannot be solved by the same consciousness that created it." The world requires a new way of leading. Conscious leading provides a new way and it just needs you to decide that you want to change and follow through in making it happen. Mahatma Gandhi said it best when he said, "You must be the change you want to see in the world." Your decision point is either to continue doing the same things and expecting a different result, as Einstein stated: "The definition of insanity is doing the same thing, over and over again, but expecting different results," or decide to change and take actions to achieve it. This guide is about taking action to be the change you want to see. The decision is yours.

You have now decided to be the change you want to see in the world and you are ready to begin. The first step is to define success for you. This exercise is called Future Pace. The intent is to define what success in the future looks like. Close your eyes and take three slow deep breaths. Imagine you are in the future three years from now and you are being interviewed by your favorite program, magazine or famous personality you have wanted to meet for the longest time. The interviewer is proclaiming the change you have made in your life, for your family, friends or organization is amazing and what did you do to achieve it? Picture or get a sense of what changed and how did you do it. Stay with this picture as long as you can and look at it in different ways. How does it feel, how would you explain it to a loved one and what made the difference? It may help you to write the article answering these questions. What would the title of this feature or article be? How were you able to measure and know along your journey you were achieving this amazing change? The idea here is to start the pace toward what your future success will look like to you.

To lead others you first have to lead yourself. This means doing the internal work on you to see the change in others. Expecting the world to change without you changing will not happen. The internal change required is becoming consciously aware of what is going on in your life, the choices and decisions you are making and the results you are getting. This simple formula will drive your personal transformation. A number of steps in Chapters 1–3 have been covered that provide many exercises to help you with your personal transformation of becoming more aware. The more aware you are, the better choices and decisions you will make, leading to different results. Success is in observing the results to determine if they are giving you what you really want. If not, make a change in actions taken by you until the results you want to have are achieved. We have also covered how to manage the most essential power source you have, which is your personal energy, in Chapter 1. Managing your energy is the fuel to energize you daily and maintains the changes you have made.

What does a new way of leading others look like? Imagine the best leader you have ever worked for. What did she or he do that made them the best? How did they treat everyone they met? What made them special? Thomas is a leader who does both very well – being a conscious leader while managing his career and pursuing his goals. I met Thomas Winter for the first time seven years ago when I interviewed and joined his new team he was forming. Focusing on doing his craft well, Thomas was a firm leader who expected results and held people accountable. His famous saying in the team was, "Who does what by when?" He was a living example of: I (innovative thinking) + T (thought provoking) + PR (proven results) = HP (high potential). He did all three very well and achieved results. His ability to get things done helped fast track him to two senior level promotions during this seven-year period. Under the surface, what made him special as a leader was his genuine care for his people and the connections he formed with his team members. The three things that stand out are:

- Making a connection with his people. He actively uses Facebook with his team to make a deeper connection with them by sharing what is going on in his life. Being in a global role with his team members spread all over the world, this helps to build personal relationships using technology, especially when you cannot see each other face to face each day. The added benefit is his actions make a positive difference for his people. This is fundamental to leading in a conscious way: connect with people and make a positive change.

- Doing the internal work to be the best you can be. Thomas attends seminars, has a coach and is a constant consumer of audio books, with the purpose to continuously improve himself and to be a better leader. This is an example of being the change you want to be and taking the actions and making time to learn and further develop.

- Giving feedback that moves people and makes a difference. Thomas has an ability that the majority of leaders lack or do not have the confidence to try, which is to give real feedback about what is possibly holding you back. I covered earlier the story of the feedback he gave me on what could be holding me back from my next promotion when he asked me: "Do you really want it? And do you feel worthy?" Had he not provided the right message at the right time, I would not have been moved to take the action I needed for my transformation. Conscious leaders make a positive difference, and he did.

What has helped Thomas to become an example of being a conscious leader? Thomas says, "My journey has been one of not being attached and being playful. Take things lightly. I check my fear and have confidence I am making a difference." Thomas gives people respect and does not fear asking stupid questions. What helped Thomas make the change is his first boss was all about "do what I say." This poor example had the positive impact to show Thomas how he did not want to do it. He added: "There are things I saw my father do and I made a firm decision I would never say or do that and today those decisions still hold." So the bad example can actually create a positive if you can see it for the learning that it provides.

Another big shift for Thomas came from doing the work he needed to do in order to clear beliefs that were impacting his life. Knowing yourself and working on your opportunities brings an element of effectiveness to your life. Thomas worked on what Seth Godin calls the lizard brain in his book *Linchpin*. He looked at what drives the lizard brain, or emotional brain, or limbic brain. What behaviors were generating the way he was acting in his life? Fear was a critical element. The four shifts he had:

- Accept and respect the senior person. Thomas made peace with the fact they are the boss. If you have thoughts or feel like I expect a leader to be X or do Y, I am smarter than them, I am entitled to Z, these are mental patterns that will show up when you speak or interact with them. Paul Ekman (www.paulekman. com), an expert on human non-verbal communication identified that there are more than 10,000 discrete human facial expressions. These different expressions can generate a subconscious response in the person we are communicating with. Ben who is a mid-level executive believes he should have been promoted to the next level already and feels deep down inside himself he is better than his boss. Because he has this program running at the subconscious level his communication with his boss is filled with examples of where his boss is not good enough and he continues to expose his boss to the point where his leader does not feel good. The one who suffers is Ben, as he does not realize he is doing this and setting himself up to fail. These are the subconscious beliefs to become aware of. If you do and then make the shift like Thomas did, then freedom awaits you and the rest will fall into position.

- Both people can be right, there does not have to be a winner in every conversation. Abandon the thought that there has to be one winner and find the common denominator between the two of you. In his experience there is always a common point you both can agree on.

- Being comfortable with where he is. When he looks at going to the next level he does this with conscious thought. He asks the key questions to himself like what do I get more or different if I take that position? For example, Thomas has made the decision to stick with his values and not relocate. He has decided his family and way of living is what he wants most now in his life. This is key as many just get caught in "I have to get the next role" without realizing the impacts it can have on them and their family. The key is he makes a conscious choice and then accepts it without second guessing his decisions.

- Having kids creates an opportunity to reflect on what is really important in your life. They give you an opportunity to deal with life. This becomes a development catalyst for you. My two big development catalysts: my experience being in the military and hearing my two-year-old say no. What a learning opportunity!

Thomas did the work he needed to do attending seminars on Systemic Constellation, which is a therapeutic intervention with roots in family systems therapy. This allowed him to address the baggage he had about authority and his mother's life choices. He found he was tied to his limiting beliefs and wanted to determine why he acted in a certain way. The training gave him the opportunity to reflect and determine why he behaved the way he did to certain situations. This created a paradigm shift. The focus was on the family environment and looking at the accusations, being able to forgive and redirect the flow of energy. They did the best they could with where they were in their development and life choices. He had physical symptoms with arthritis until he was able to accept the path his mother had taken, even though it made her sick. The acceptance and being able to let it go made the difference. His physical symptoms disappeared and he was free.

Conscious leaders are willing to do what they believe is right, regardless of what others think, to take their people and themselves to higher levels and make a difference. In sports we see evolutionary breakthroughs to improve performance steadily and allow athletes to compete for much longer, faster than in the corporate world. We expect our athletes to do whatever it takes to perform at their best and have very low expectations that employees will do the same rigorous disciplined activities to be their best every day. Sir Clive Woodward is an example of a leader using different approaches to raise the performance of his players and this resulted in the success of England winning the 2003 Rugby World Cup. In his book *Winning!* he explains what he called the "critical non-essentials," where he and his leaders wanted to set playing for the England national team apart from the players' own clubs by making the experience of playing on the team unique. Their goal was to make the experience so special that no one would want to be left out from being part of it. One of these "critical non-essentials" was bringing Dr. Sherylle Calder on board to help the players improve their sports vision by training their eyes. What she had observed is the biggest opportunities in either the defense or offense was the players being able to see correctly the space on the rugby pitch. Most players were not looking up unless they had the ball in their hands. They needed to create the habit in the players of continually looking around the pitch throughout the game. One approach they deployed was to hang banners while training that had the three letters CTC, which stood for Crossbar, Touchline, and Communicate. This became a new vision standard for the team. During the game players were required to look continually at the crossbar, look at each touchline on the side of the pitch, while communicating their position to others. Based on the training they did, the team was rarely out of position and this was one contributing factor to England winning the title. The essential takeaway is Sir Clive Woodward made a positive difference by wanting to create a special experience for each of his players and he was willing to do something out of the ordinary by bringing an eye coach to his staff to achieve a unique result.

A conscious leader embraces new approaches, different paradigms and ideas to fill their leader's toolkit with a variety of options they can use. The leader is willing to practice and play with the tools to make a difference for helping the people they are entrusted to lead make the shifts they need to expand and grow. The right tool at the right time can have a profound impact on removing performance blocks, stress or anything that gets in the person's way. Patrick who is a physical therapist embraces new methods of treating his clients to get them back into action as soon as possible. He has helped me on a number of occasions be able to compete in a marathon race by deploying some of these tools in his toolkit, be it either using electrical current or acupuncture to help an overused muscle to recover faster. His work with a young Olympic level gymnast who fell during a routine and injured herself was a clear example of helping overcome a performance block by deploying a tool from his toolkit. The tool he used was Emotional Freedom Techniques (EFT), which I covered in more detail in Chapter 3. A quick reminder is EFT is a tool that can help you address the emotions and beliefs that are tied to a past event. The young gymnast was emotionally connected to the injury. Patrick could treat the injury itself, however the next time she would attempt to do the same routine she was doing when she was injured, the emotions she experienced as a result of the injury were still there. Patrick began to use EFT with her to clear the emotion she had around the event injury. As soon as he started, her heart was racing, her breathing became rapid and she was fully associated back into the event. He could physically see she was feeling the emotions from the incident. Using EFT with her had the desired result. She was able to release the emotions that she had been feeling and was able to look at the event now for the learning to be gained. The performance block was removed so she could get back into her routine without bringing the emotions back up from the event when she had fallen.

Imagine the application that a tool like EFT could do for you and others you are helping. An account manager goes on a sales call or customer visit and for some reason it does not go well, reaching no deal. It is possible that he or she unconsciously associates negative emotions to the event or some aspect of the event. These aspects are called triggers and can be a sound, a person's face, or a certain way of being touched or anything in the environment. The account manager goes out on their next sales opportunity and the emotional baggage from every other meeting they had in the past comes with them. If they do not get this sale, this can lead to even more potential baggage, creating a slump. Typical responses are: You'll get the next one, hang in there and keep trying; your ship will come in soon. Will they be able on their own to just get over it? It is possible and by putting in the increased number of visits the odds are a number of sales can be achieved. Is this good enough for them or the company? What if they were able to release anything that is blocking them from making a sale on every visit, by taking their emotional blocked baggage out of the equation? Would this be of value to them and the company? The new way of leading others is about helping them unlock their full potential by helping them to get out of the way of themselves. Conscious leading in the workplace is treating people like a world class athlete for the entire time they are with you. Bringing out the best in them to make the difference they want to achieve in their lives.

Those things that keep getting in your way of changing

Making the initial change and sustaining the change you want to have in your life are your two biggest inhibitors to being successful with your conscious transformation. Why is change difficult even when your life-long happiness is at stake? Aristotle highlights our habits play a factor when he says, "We are what we repeatedly do. Excellence therefore is not an action, but a habit." Our habits can set us up for success or get in our way of making the changes we want to be. Habits and those programs running at the subconscious level make up 95% of what we do, with only 5% coming from being conscious. These programs include such things as controlling our breathing, digestion and learned behaviors such as when you learn to drive a car, at first you have to concentrate on the steps to drive and when you have done it over and over again, it becomes a habit that you do not consciously have to think about every time you drive a car. It is easier to stay the same than changing. It is as though we have seen the enemy – the enemy is us. The number one thing to getting in our way of change is our self. This could be our beliefs, habits or that little voice that keeps us from taking action today to put it off till tomorrow. This guide has been designed to give you more awareness of what is blocking you and give you tools and ideas to overcome the resistance to change. It comes down to taking charge of your transformation and taking the steps to make it a reality.

Imagine a ship traveling along in the water. You see the part of the ship above the waterline and not the part below. The things above the waterline are most visible and decisions made above the waterline such as the type and arrangement of the deck furniture, placement of the lifeboats, flag location or color scheme will not sink the boat. Decisions taken below the waterline can sink the boat. Some people will argue that the visible part is where you should focus, because this is the most visible and if it looks good no one will look deeper. In the military this is where painting the rocks outside the barracks became so important for inspection, because the belief was if it looks good they will not look deeper. And besides, who cares how the engine room looks? Some people focus their lives on this same principle, make the exterior look good and I will be successful. Wear the best clothing, focus on external things in the hope that this will make them feel happy and fulfilled. The challenge is that this is temporary and does not give people the real happiness they seek. This also invites habits of excess shopping, excess eating or drinking, watching endless TV, gambling or other activity to achieve the feeling they seek. This can lead to greater excess as betting $50 no longer gives one the same feeling, so now they bet $100 and so forth. Real happiness comes from within and those things under the waterline. This is the internal work, which is where real transformation occurs. Thus the second thing that gets in your way of changing is not doing the internal work and focusing on the external possessions and stimulus as your primary means of being happy.

The third area that gets in your way of making the change and having it stick is not having an approach to follow or not understanding what combination of items will create the change you are looking to achieve. Using a systematic approach can aid you in achieving the result you want to have. A system can be used as a planning or troubleshooting tool for a plan you are already implementing. First choose the result you want to achieve. What is the reason you want that result? This is your purpose, and the greater your desire and the intensity of emotion you can put into why you want it, the more you will be motivated to having it. The key here is building your desire for wanting your result. Next you will look at the set-up of your system you are creating, which means do you have the items you need to be successful? This can include having the right equipment, knowing when and how to use it, having a support network or someone who can help you like a friend, coach or mentor, and knowing what you expect from yourself to achieve your result. With having the set-up complete or in place, you will want to establish the reward to drive you to achieve the result. Having no reward or a punishing reward for doing the right thing will not lead to achieving what you want. The last item to complete your system is building in a review mechanism to ensure you are getting what you want and to make changes to your plan until you do. For example, if John's goal is to qualify for the Boston Marathon, he would need to have a qualification time for the 40- to 44-year-old men's age group of 3:15 or faster. His purpose could be for charity to make a difference, to achieve a goal of running one of the five major marathons (which include Boston, Berlin, London, Chicago and New York) or another reason. The set-up would include his running kit, training and resources to set him up to achieve this time in a qualifying marathon within the timeline required by the Boston Marathon Association. John could pick any reward that he knows is significant enough to him to drive his motivation to do the work to achieve the result. This could be a week's vacation to some location he wants to visit, a personal feeling of achievement or another reward. For the review mechanism he can use a premade training calendar, use a running watch or established pre-races to see if he is hitting his expected times. He idea is he approaches achieving the result he wants by applying a system approach. This greatly enhances the likelihood of making the change he wants.

The fourth area that blocks change is fear. Fear takes many forms: fear of the unknown, fear that others will not want to be with them if they change too much or any fear beliefs that hold them in their current situation. Some create their entire identity around their personal victim story, their illness, their pain and their whatever they have told themselves over and over and now believe this is who they are story. They believe if they change and no longer have this story, the fear of the unknown derails their change efforts. One way leaders fall victim to the fear trap is by the need to control everything, believing this controls their own destiny. By wanting to control everything they limit the growth of their people and rarely collaborate with others to bring a better solution or result to the situation. These leaders end up in a set-up to fail cycle they have created themselves, as the results either miss on the expectations or are not as good had they collaborated with others. The leader's brand is impacted and this then impacts their career. Thus their fear drove them to be more controlling, leading to a poorer solution and the fear is still experienced by the action they took to do it alone. Conducting a fear inventory is an exercise you can use to understand your fears better. On a piece of paper or in your journal take as much time as you need and answer the following questions: What do I have a fear of? What situations keep coming up in my life that I do not want or like? What fear do I have that can be causing this to keep coming up? The intent of these questions is to give you awareness of fears that will impact on your ability to change or sustain the change. You may resonate with some of these fears: fear of failure, not being accepted, not being liked by others, not being worthy, judgment, being embarrassed, standing out, spending money on yourself, how you look, or public speaking. The exercises throughout this book have been set up to bring more insight into the fears you have and tools to assist you in overcoming them.

The fifth area is learning and knowing your identity, the strengths you have and the pitfalls that come with it. Your identity is who you are and the idea is to gain as much expertise and understanding as you can about how you work best. It will be difficult to achieve a change that does not match who you are. It would be like a 380-pound American football offense lineman wanting to be a track and field pole-vaulter while staying the same weight. They will try and try and not be very successful at it and may give up entirely. The giving up creates momentum in the opposite direction. Stop once and it gets easier and easier to stop a second and a third time and this then becomes a continuous cycle of try, give up, stop, on to the next thing and same cycle repeats. Knowing yourself helps to accentuate your natural strengths to support setting yourself up for success. Tools that can help you to understand your natural strengths better include: Link-up International's Instinctive Drives, Myer-Briggs Type Indicator (MBTI), StrengthsFinder 2.0 from Gallup and others.

Paul Burgess' book *Natural Born Success* explains what the drives are and the process of identifying your Instinctive Drives. His company offers the opportunity for your organization, self and family to discover your profiles. Your Instinctive Drives is about what motivates you to do the things you do. There are four drives that make up your profile: Verify, Authenticate, Complete and Improvise. After you complete the questionnaire you will receive a report that explains your I.D. and covers your natural talents, natural vulnerabilities and relevant strategies to assist you with the vulnerabilities. The strength of using a tool like Instinctive Drives is you understand better what motivates and does not motivate you. One of my Instinctive Drive needs is for unconditional acceptance and unconditional encouragement. An environment or working situation where I need to justify and explain myself constantly greatly impacts my energy and I feel drained. This is key information to know what to avoid if I'm looking to drive a change in my life. In addition, these insights provide great advantages in a work environment. If each member already knows what drives the other team members, the time needed to reach effective work relationships is shortened. For example, Todd was leading a group of managers and when he gave the guidance to his team he would give them information based on his natural tendencies. He was surprised when the leaders kept coming back and asking more questions to get more detail. After he and his team completed their Instinctive Drives profiles, he realized his team manager's needs were opposite to his in one of the areas. He was able to adjust quickly, leading to better communications and results. The idea is the better you know yourself, the better your success when driving changes in your life.

Key Points

Your takeaway from this chapter is a new paradigm for leading in a conscious way, being an example for others. Together we covered:

- Impact of old-school leadership practices on people and an organization.

- Conscious leading and the ability to enjoy the journey on the way up the mountain, while you also enjoy the success of accomplishing your goals.

- Melissa Rancourt was profiled on how she does both well.

- In a new way of leading others you learned about future pacing, which is defining what success looks like to you.

- To lead others you first have to lead yourself. Your success formula starts with becoming aware, making different choices or decisions based on this new awareness and this leads to different results.

- We covered examples of what leading others looks like. Three things that stood out about Thomas were: making a connection with people, doing the internal work to be the best you can be and giving feedback that moves people and makes a difference.

- Sir Clive Woodward provides an example of using different approaches to raise performance. His "critical non-essentials" were a key enabling element to England's 2003 Rugby World Cup championship.

- A conscious leader embraces new approaches to add more tools to their leader's toolkit. One such tool is Emotional Freedom Techniques (EFT) with a description of how its applications remove blocks preventing change for you and your workforce.

- Regarding things that get in your way of changing we covered:

  o Habits and subconscious programs run 95% of what we do with only 5% driving our conscious actions.

  o The internal work or those things below the waterline on a ship in the water is where the real transformation, fulfillment and happiness occur.

  o Use a systematic approach to aid in the achievement of the results you want in your life.

  o Fear has a significant impact on your ability to change and sustain the changes. Use the fear inventory to create awareness and learn more about what you fear. This helps to bring you more visibility and focus to your development actions.

  o Knowing your identity, strengths and pitfalls to set yourself up for success is important to ensure you are on the right seat on the bus or the right bus to be successful with your transformation. Tools such as Instinctive Drives help to give you a richer picture of what motivates you and how to use the information best to support you on your journey.

CHAPTER 7

Leadership Guide To Transformation

Being a conscious leader

"All your dreams can come true – if we have the courage to pursue them." – Walt Disney.

Thus far we have discussed your conscious transformation work. By doing the inner work you have the foundation to now work on being a transformational leader. The inner work is a constant and is one of the defining characteristics of a transformational leader. A transformational leader is someone who is a change agent and helps others to be moved or have a shift that makes a positive change occur in their lives. The highest level of the impact a transformational leader can have is once they are able to help a person grow, that person goes on to help even more people grow. This generates an amazing sustaining cycle of giving and has the biggest organizational and societal impact for creating a new paradigm of leading. Most forgettable leaders have adopted the maladaptive habits of former weak leaders; they are a product of limited to poor examples. The transformational leader becomes the example by choice and is consciously aware that their actions speak louder than words and they are congruent with the example they provide. They are very consistent in every aspect of their life and embody the concepts of conscious leading. The transformational leader has the courage to pursue their dreams and help others pursue and achieve theirs. This chapter is about being a transformational leader and providing a guide to help you achieve it.

Do forgettable leaders give up before they start due to expectations, which seem, in their mind, to be unrealistic? Are forgettable leaders reluctant to sign up for the responsibility that comes with being a leader? This marks the key difference between having a title that calls you a leader to really being a leader. The optimum word here is being. Being is about making the inner choice that you are a leader and having the courage to step fully into all the aspects of leadership and becoming a master at doing it. The type of leader we most want to be around is the one who has taken the plunge to being a leader and not one on paper. The four leaders who I have had the honor to work for who I would work for again in a second were all leaders who made the choice to be a leader and took the actions to be entirely the best they could. The by-product is they became transformational leaders by the nature of consciously deciding they wanted to be great at being a leader. The big idea and key is a transformational leader chooses to be a leader and to be the best they can at doing it. The leader model we introduced in Chapter 5 of "master being a leader, master your craft and master yourself" is an approach to focus your development on these essential three areas and support your transition to becoming a transformational leader.

To master being a transformational leader it is essential to know the competencies to focus on. Competencies define the qualities that qualify one to be a transformational leader. How well you understand, apply, use, rehearse and master these competencies is the equation you bring and establishes how good you will be as a leader. The top 10 transformational leader competencies to be a change agent and help others to be moved or have a shift that makes a positive change occur in their lives include:

1. ***Care deeply for others.*** The number one competency is the care for people. A transformational leader cares more for their people's success than their own. They check their ego at the door and wake up every morning thinking about what they can do today for the best of their team and people. They do it because they love helping others. They care and want to see people succeed by getting the best out of themselves, when they may have even doubted they could do it. The reward is happiness and making a difference in people's lives for the better.

2. ***Lead by example.*** The leader does what they say they will do. They will do the right thing every time, even if it is unpopular or regardless of the circumstances. He or she is willing to do the things they are asking others to do. They will get their hands dirty. These elements build trust and willingness by others to follow your decisions and advice.

*3. **Create breakthroughs and disrupt for lasting change.*** Here a transformational leader provides compassionate and from the heart feedback that moves a person from an undesired to a desired state. The delivery of the message is presented in a way that inspires the individual to action. Courage is an integral characteristic of a transformational leader to create positive disruption. They call out what is not working, challenge the status quo, challenge legacy and productively drive change to make improvements. This helps to clear roadblocks that allow team members to break through the things preventing them from succeeding. The leader inspects and make corrections where required to continue the positive move forward.

*4. **Does the continued work on themselves.*** Being free from your own blocks, judgment, fears, limiting beliefs and other past event emotions is an ongoing process. Like peeling an onion, as a person frees energy by releasing an element that is holding them to their past, yet another layer of learning is exposed and available. Taking the action to be committed to doing the work on yourself builds your confidence and provides first-hand stories from your experience to help others see possible alternatives.

*5. **Influence for betterment of the person.*** The transformational leader is able to remove their own ego, beliefs and judgments when influencing a person to change. The change is for the betterment of the person they are helping, given the situation and circumstance that person is having in their life. Influence causes a shift that expands their world and the highest level is when the leader is able to influence someone to influence others for the greater good.

*6. **Master their skills.*** To help others change, a transformational leader must master the skills of change, coaching, communication, giving feedback, displaying empathy, questioning, listening and their toolkit of tools and techniques they will use to guide and help others. The leader is committed to learning, practicing and using new tools and techniques to expand their toolkit. The leader knows the value of coaching and mentoring and has their own coach and mentor to continue their own learning.

7. ***Has "I am a leader" attitude.*** The leader embraces their role of being a leader and is comfortable with the responsibility it brings. They see themselves as a steward of the talent they are leading, which means their role is to prepare and help them to advance beyond their current role and team. They help people see the possibilities and inspire them to reach for and achieve those opportunities. They accomplish this by creating a compelling and shared vision. They align the vision both inside and outside the organization to facilitate accomplishing it.

8. ***Build a trusting environment.*** Trustworthiness is a must characteristic of a transformational leader and is the essential ingredient to build an environment where people feel safe. If a person does not feel safe or does not trust the leader, anything they do will be seen with suspicion and be ineffective. The leader establishes open and transparent communication with the team and each member to build trust. The leader listens and learns about each person to establish rapport. Rapport is extremely important for the person you are trying to help to take on board the information and feedback you are providing them.

9. ***Lead people through change.*** As a transformational leader the ability to initiate and effectively guide your team and people through change is vital to helping create shifts and move people. Understanding the concept of change stages and how they interconnect from works of John P. Kotter in *Leading Change* is fundamental. Knowing how people react to change using the change curve is an effective tool to understand where people are in their journey through change and how best to support them. Effective change helps the person see the benefits of doing things differently. It installs the new behavior by aiding the transition and addresses the emotions the person is going through to give up the old behavior to adopt the new one.

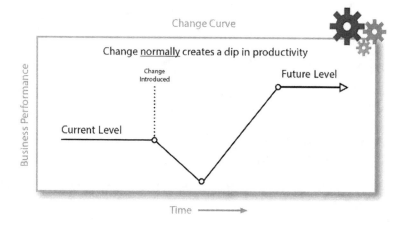

10. ***Build supporting networks.*** A transformational leader realizes networks are powerful and builds networks of mutual support and benefit to facilitate greater change. Connecting with others and building a community allows access to more options, tools, expertise, knowledge and support to develop greater solutions for the overall betterment of all the community members. This open sharing of information and connection builds more energy and excitement to drive bigger breakthroughs for all involved.

The foundational component to develop and master the top 10 transformational leader's competencies is the psychographics that are a must have to start with. A transformational leader has integrity, courage, confidence, openness, trustworthiness, humility, high energy, the ability to inspire others and is ethical. These characteristics are the base-line items that a transformational leader must have. If one of these is lacking, the leader's effectiveness and ability to lead others to change will be greatly impacted. Another way to view these is they are the non-negotiable characteristics. These are the first and most important development areas for leaders who are not demonstrating excellence in any one or more of these characteristics.

Being a transformational leader is about doing. They do the things that enable them to be successful helping others. This is a list of the things the leader does:

- They show up in the right state for the situation. State is your mood, energy level, physiology, eye contact and use of your voice.

A leader matches their state to fit the situation.

- Build rapport constantly with others.

- Set standards for others through their actions, decisions and behaviors.

- Consistent with their actions and temperament.

- Follow-through with what they said they would do and when they said they would do it.

- Continuous improvement focused on bettering themselves, others and their team.

- Listen to understand the other person's point fully and with compassion.

- Manage their energy by mastering the elements of their energy management system.

- Give time away freely to support their people.

A transformational leader looks at the near, mid and long-term for planning actions and initiatives to build the skills they and their team need, while also building capabilities for their organization. Initiatives, activities and projects that are being worked on today will be the strengths of the team and company in two to three years. A visual way to help in planning is the three horizons tool, which are short-term, mid-term and long-term actions that you or your team will focus your development on. The three horizons consist of:

- **Horizon one:** These are the tactical skills or activities that occur or are a one-year focus effort.

- **Horizon two:** This is the transition to the strategic phase and is those elements that build the mid-term skills to enable the longer term ones. The timeframe is normally between 12–24 months.

- **Horizon three:** The strategic skills and activities to realize the strategic direction or vision the transformational leader wants to achieve. The timeframe is normally three to five years.

The purpose again is to provide a visual map of the next five years of skills and activities to be accomplished to keep the focus at the forefront of what you are looking to achieve. This brings simplicity and ease of quick periodic review to keep focus and momentum flowing toward attainment. The diagram below provides an example of how a development three-horizon map could look like.

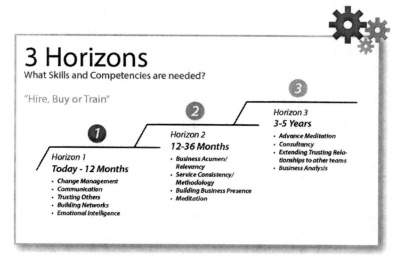

To build out the type of activities to complete your development plan there are a few approaches that can be helpful. The first is breaking activities into three groups: Exposure, Education and Experience. Exposure tends to be 20% of your development activities and is about learning through others. Experience is the biggest opportunity for development and would normally be about 70% of your activities and the focus is on learning by doing a role. The last area making up 10% is education and learning by attending courses. Prior to gaining experience using all three I tended to rely heavily on education through reading and attending courses. The more I incorporated the other two in my development, my skills improved and I picked up more practical knowledge in different ways to apply what I learned in the classroom. Here are some examples of the three Es:

- **Exposure:** Find a mentor, participate in events or clubs, join a network, and shadow a person who already has the skills, meet with peers to share best practices.

- **Education:** Attending courses, workshops, seminars, webinars, podcasts, reading books etc.

- **Experience:** On the job training (OJT), volunteering for assignments and projects, practicing and rehearsing techniques you have learned, journaling etc.

Another approach is to build your program from a position of your strengths and things you enjoy. There are tools we used to learn more about what motivates and further helps identify how you best work, such as Link-up International's Instinctive Drives, Myer-Briggs Type Indicator (MBTI), StrengthsFinder 2.0 from Gallup and others. In Chapter 1 on peak energy, in the exercise on things that juice you, we covered how to find those things that give you energy by identifying the things you enjoy and the things you do not. This approach follows the concept of building a program that sets you up for success. If you dread your program and are not inspired you will not follow through and will not achieve the results you are looking for. Making the program fun and building it around things you enjoy greatly enhances your ability to maintain and continue with the program.

Being a transformational leader begins with having the courage to pursue your dreams and making the choice to make a difference for your people and the world. It is about having the core psychographics, mastering the top 10 competencies, and doing the things that enable you to help others. All of this is achievable and within your reach by building a sustainable development program over the three horizons with activities leveraging exposure, education and experience. Making it fun and leveraging your natural strengths enhances the success that you will stick with the program to obtain the results you seek. The ingredient to move the plan to results is disciplined execution.

Your transformational leader's playbook

A playbook gives you the plays and scripts to practice until they become second nature. It is designed to ensure consistent execution and once learned to perfection, leads to mastery. In the U.S. military we would create our standard operating procedures (SOP) and battle drills to make it easier to execute on common tasks or situations we would most likely encounter in a combat situation. Each solider and unit is drilled and practices these procedures over and over to make them a habit to where you do not have to think about them to execute it. It becomes part of you and how you operate. As I mentioned earlier, in Desert Storm when I was operating under limited sleep and running on my own adrenalin, the habit of learning these drills came to me without having to think consciously about them. After one firefight and in order to secure the enemy fighting position, I needed to enter the makeshift bunker. The intelligence we had was the enemy was booby-trapping positions and equipment to cause injury and death. With this in my mind and without thought before entering the position, I naturally began executing the battle drill for searching for trip wires as I had been trained and practiced many, many, many times before. The big idea is using this same concept of creating your own transformational leader drills. Practicing them over and over again builds the habit and makes them part of who you are. As your confidence grows so does your courage and energy – a huge added benefit.

Another active concept in the military was to build continuity binders. These binders were designed to capture the knowledge of how certain parts of the job were done and pass these on to the next person who took your role. This helped them get up to speed more quickly by having the information already available. There are a number of knowledge capture or process flow documentation tools that accomplish this. The concept to take away is by capturing your knowledge on how you do something brings greater awareness to how you do things. This awareness brings clarity to success patterns you have already that you can leverage to other parts of your life. The awareness allows you to assess whether the current process is the best way, or is there an even better way? The act of capturing your knowledge, success routines and how you do things makes you more conscious of how you work best and identify areas to add to your playbook. The goal is to build a playbook or collection of material to reference, practice and master to make success habits to support your transformation best and help others make their shifts.

What would a transformational leader's playbook look like? Think of this as a collection of things you want to remember, learn, use as motivation, guide you when you need a reference or to simply inspire you. When I was an army officer I had my knowledge book always with me on every exercise in my hip pocket or day pack. In this book, which I still have today, I had references to things I needed most or those one-off events that occasionally would come up. For example, I would use the army five paragraph operations order format cards when I was tired to ensure I did not forget any critical information when planning the next operation. I would have information on the steps to the best way to have critical conversations as a drill to rehearse until it became a habit. It would also include things such as load planning for helicopter operations. Today my playbook includes pictures, quotes, articles, key takeaways from books, blogs, articles and how to drills on things like quick guides to negotiations and others. For me the act of writing it down, cutting the picture out or adding it to my book helps me to remember it better. My playbook also includes my goals for the next five years, my code of conduct, values, commitments, life plan and completed exercises to the ones in this book. I review these on a weekly basis to ensure I am on track with what I want and to plan my week to accomplish the most important things for that week. Your playbook would include anything that you find useful and best supports you. There is no rigid format, so have fun with it and build one that works for you.

Tools that support a transformational leader

Throughout this book I have included a number of tools that will support you in your personal transformation and can be used to support you as a transformational leader. In this section we cover the importance of planning, self-reflection, mindset, Neuro-Linguistic Programing (NLP) basics to understand people better, and using questions. These are tools to add to your transformational leader's toolkit to help you with supporting others in achieving the changes they want in their life.

Tool: Planning. When I was training to be a U.S. army ranger we spent hours in the planning bays to prepare for executing our missions. This time was extremely valuable as the planning and then rehearsals paid off every time by ensuring we were ready to do what we planned for and prepared us for a multiple number of contingencies that could occur. The saying we used to refer to is, "your plan goes out the window once the first shot is fired." Planning and preparing for contingencies becomes a valuable tool to help you be prepared for those things that can happen in your environment that can throw you off track and derail your plan. Contingency planning builds confidence that you are ready for the top things that could go wrong and are ready to respond if they do occur. This is empowering for the people you are helping. They can create routines, which can counter the things that could impact the action plans they built to drive change in their life. To build your contingencies, first list all the possible things that could happen. Next prioritize your list by rating each item on your list from one to 10, with one being a low chance it could occur to 10 being a high chance it could occur. Pick the top five and do the following:

1. Take one item at a time and determine what is the most likely reason that could cause the issue to happen.

2. What actions can you do upfront that could reduce that risk from happening?

3. Take the actions that can prevent those causes you identified from occurring.

4. By doing the above you reduce risk of the top issues from occurring. The challenge can still occur, so what can you do to ensure you have awareness if the issue does happen anyway? What notification system or mechanism can you put in place to make you aware that it has happened?

5. If the problem occurs, what contingency actions can you take to minimize the impact and get you back on track with your plan?

6. Rehearse the actions mentally or physically to be prepared and give yourself more confidence in your plan of action.

Tool: Self-reflection.

The ability to review your actions, behaviors and what is happening in your life brings clarity and awareness. The most important thing it brings is wisdom and new insights. This is a daily or weekly exercise you can do in your journal, with people you are helping or an entire team. With my leadership team in our Monday leaders' meeting I will ask each member what they learned last week. This reflection helps them to look at what wisdom they gained from the events of the last week and helps me to learn and see what perspective they are using to review and reflect. In the military we would incorporate feedback sessions at the end of every mission and training exercise to build a reflection culture of constant learning from what went well and what didn't go so well. When working with others, using self-reflection helps them to identify patterns of things working and not working. It allows them to learn key lessons that they can apply to their plan or success routines. Questions such as: What did you learn from that event? What knowledge did you gain from the conversation you had with them? What decision did you make at that time? And other questions can be used.

⏣ Tool: Mindset.

Understanding the mental framework you or the person is using is essential for creating opportunities for shift. All advice, coaching and guidance can be helpful if the person is receptive. It takes the right advice at the right time to be heard and understood by the right person at the right time. Without this connection it tends to be a nice conversation but shifts rarely happen. As the person giving the advice, not being fully vested in the outcome is an important mindset to adopt. Quieting your internal judge and critic is vital, so you maintain your openness to all alternatives and are able to listen truly to what they are telling you. If you listen, their words will tell you all their limiting beliefs and you then can best help them. The biggest mindset shift is moving from the victim to being empowered. In Chapter 3, in the section "What tools can you use for your transformation?" the exercise on victim mindset will help here. The main components to mindset as a tool are how you show up with your mindset as the helper, listening to what they are really saying and using the victim mindset exercise to help them see another way. The shift is from being a victim to realizing you are accountable and responsible for everything you get in life.

⏣ Tool: Neuro-Linguistic Programing (NLP) basics to understand people better.

NLP provides many powerful tools that you can use for shifting behaviors and making change happen in your life. I highly recommend you take a course and start by reading *Introducing NLP* by Joseph O'Connor and John Seymour. The focus on this tool is the better you can understand people, the better you will build rapport and notice changes in them. Communication consists of three parts: words only being normally 7% of the message, tonality being 38% and physiology being 55%. With the words they use being only 7%, noticing changes in their tonality and use of their body is important. These changes can include facial expressions, eye movement, changes in their breathing, posture, gestures, tone, volume, tempo and skin tone. Each is a sign to help you know if the tools or techniques you are helping them with are working. In NLP one technique for building rapport is called matching and mirroring. The idea is to mirror and match the other person's words, tonality and body language. This takes practice otherwise you will look funny and will have the opposite effect and break rapport. Understanding NLP basics can help you match your message to their preferred representational system. The four preferred styles I will briefly cover here are visual, auditory, kinesthetic and auditory digital from my work with NLP Master Lynda Dyer.

- **Visual:** Example words the person would use if this is their preferred system: see, look, view, appear, envision, imagine, picture, clear and others. These people memorize by seeing pictures and colors as important. They would tend to have trouble remembering verbal instructions.

- **Auditory:** Example words you would hear from them include: hear, listen, tone, sound, silence, tune in or out and voice an opinion. They learn by listening and sounds are important. They like to be told how they are doing and memorize sequentially.

- **Kinesthetic:** Example words they would use include: feel, do, touch, grasp, make contact, catch on and tap into. They are interested in if it feels right to them and activities are important to them. They learn and memorize by doing the task or walking through it.

- **Auditory digital:** Example words include: think, idea, experience, process, decide, consider, calculate and distinct. They are interested in if it makes sense to them and are focused on logic and the details.

✪ Tool: Questions.

A question is the most important tool in your leader's toolkit and will be used most. The right questions framed in the right way can bring instant awareness, revelations and shifts in people. Questions can bring out a person's beliefs that are holding them back and gives you the indication of where and what they need to work on. There are two types of questions: open and closed. Open questions are used open-ended and will get a deeper and more complete answer. For example, can you explain how that discussion with your partner made you feel? Closed questions solicit a yes or no answer. For example, did the discussion with your partner make you mad? Both have a purpose and can be used to get to the core of an opportunity or challenge. Closed questions will normally be used to confirm facts or points, where open questions will gain a greater understanding of the situation. What I find works best is as I find great questions I put them in my leader's playbook to use them as part of my toolkit.

These tools along with others throughout this book are to help you with your transformation and to help others with theirs. A tool is only as good as you know how to use it. Practice and mastery is essential to make this part of who you are and make it easier driving transformation.

Steps to becoming a transformational leader

Thus far we have emphasized the importance of making the choice to be a leader and this act has a profound positive impact on your mindset of being a conscious leader. The characteristics and competencies allow you the opportunity to create your development plan to ensure the core foundation is established to enable your success. Mastering your toolkit gives you the ability to help others make the changes they seek to implement. The next steps are designed to set you up for success in taking on the role of being a transformational leader who makes a difference for others. This section is about those steps and how to stack the deck in your favor to win.

Step one: Set yourself up to win. Some people set their goals so high they have to pass away to achieve them. We have discussed using tools to understand better what motivates you, your strengths, what drains you of energy and how to manage your state. These are fundamental to build a sustainable plan you can action to be successful. The plan you create and goals you set must be something you will enjoy doing. If you honestly enjoy something you will have fun doing it and this will become a success habit for you. When something is enjoyable we lose track of time and become in the flow. Things you can do to add fun is score what you are doing by adding music to it or some other form of entertainment to the event. Bring emotions to the activity and imagine the excitement of achieving your goal and make the image so real you can reach out and touch it. On the other side if you use punishment as a motivator you will have short-term gains, however you are unlikely to continue it for the longer term. Thus set up what you will be doing so it will be fun and enjoyable. Establish rewards along the way for milestones you achieve. Small changes made every day lead to major changes. By rewarding yourself along the trip you recognize the great job you are doing by keeping the discipline and following through. The most important aspect of setting yourself up to win is mastering the use of your calendar. What gets scheduled gets done. I enjoy how Leo Babauta in *Zen Habits* explains creating your "most important things (MIT)" to do and focus on the top four and forget the rest. When planning your week imagine you have seven buckets representing each day and your top four MITs are large rocks. Place the large rocks in the buckets first and do those things first in the morning of that day. The rest of the buckets will get filled with sand and small rocks, however your most important things will get done each week. Moving your goals forward by ensuring they get scheduled each week and completed is the secret sauce to setting yourself up to win.

Step two: Role models. A role model provides an example of excellence or they have a skill of doing something really well that you would like to be able to do also. The role model can be someone from history, someone you know, someone you don't know and they can be anyone. A great way to view the world is you can learn something from every person on the planet and therefore everyone is a role model for that one thing or many things they do really well. If your role model is someone who is alive and they can become a mentor to you that is even better. The questions to answer in your journal are:

- Who is your role model?

- What are the elements, traits, behaviors, actions or things they do that you admire most?

- How do you need to behave or act to be like them?

- How would you need to feel to be like them doing that activity you admire?

- What do you need to know and learn to be like them?

- What actions can you take to acquire the skill and do the same thing?

- What do you need to add to your development plan?

Step three: Build your conscious network. Doing things with others makes it more fun and greatly enhances the likelihood you will stick with it. Having a supportive network and team with you is smart to setting up yourself to be successful. When you look at great athletes they have a team around them that gets them ready to perform at their optimal level. The team normally includes a coach, public relations person, physical trainer, sports psychologist and others. I have used this same approach with my marathon training, even though I run for enjoyment, to build a team to help me perform at my best. Through research, reading, speaking with others and asking for advice from other runners and running stores, I have assembled a team that supports me. I have a specialist who provides the insoles for my shoes, one who fits and modifies my shoes to my style of running and an expert on koniology therapy for any injuries that come up. This group has had a major positive impact on my ability to keep running and improve my performance. For my spiritual or higher self-connection I have a team that consists of three coaches, my yoga instructor and a number of guided meditation and self-improvement authors. These examples are meant to demonstrate that a team approach and building your network will benefit you in building your knowledge and allow you to share and learn from others. Along your path you will meet many people and the energy you share will increase the energy you all have. Your network will quickly grow and flourish.

Step four: Know your special abilities. When you imagine a super hero like Superman, Wonder Woman or Spiderman you can define the abilities they have that make them special. This could be having spider sense or the ability to see through things. Everyone has special abilities. Knowing your special abilities gives you a platform to contribute to help others. Your special skills are already a strength of yours and the easiest to master, because you are already good at them. Advertise your strengths and use them to help others learn how to be better at what you do well already. With the many groups available on social media, reaching out and contributing helps you to become a known expert and further develop your knowledge through interacting with others who have an interest in your area of strength. The best way to start is in your journal, create an inventory of your special abilities by thinking about them and writing them down.

Step five: Collaboration. Connecting with others and exchanging like interest increases your energy, knowledge and builds new opportunities that did not exist before. The examples such as people collaborating to create Wikipedia, or the Choice Point Movement where people contribute to work on world solutions collectively to create a better world, demonstrate that collaboration brings more solutions to address the challenges and opportunities all of us face. Collaboration brings people together and by doing so can create a new movement to drive even greater change and shifts in people. For the transformational leader, collaboration increases the resources that are available to help you and expands your ability to help others. Start your own group or search for groups that share an interest with you and begin collaborating.

Step six: *Take risk*. Risk taking is about being willing to stretch yourself to play big and get you out of your comfort zone. It is easy to do nothing and stay the way you are. No judgment here, this is fine if this is what you want. Being a transformational leader is all about driving change in you and others. To drive change you will need to do things that make your hands sweat. Asking others to change when you do not demonstrate the same willingness and you do not have the examples will not build trust or respect that you walk the talk. It is essential to do those things that are difficult and stretch you. You build knowledge, courage and confidence by doing it. We discussed in the last session the tool of contingency planning to help limit risk and be prepared to respond if the risk appears. You still take the risk and stack the odds in your favor. Make risk taking one of your weekly to do actions, by doing something that stretches you and makes your palms sweat. This has the added benefit of going after your fears, and as you see the worst case didn't happen when you took action, the hold the fear belief has diminishes. One statement that stands out in my discussion with Melissa Rancourt who I highlighted in Chapter 6 on advice she has for others on their conscious leader journey is, "Always remember that uncertainty and challenge will present itself in expected and unexpected ways. How you deal with these situations is what makes you who you are. Life is not what happens to you. Life is what you make of it."

Step seven: *Virtual avatar.* Build your avatar or persona of what a transformational leader would be like. Your goal is to make this picture as detailed and real as you can. Your avatar becomes your virtual training partner. When using my Garmin sports watch, I have the ability to run against or with my virtual running partner. The idea is I set the pace I want to be training at and I can track my performance against the virtual training partner. This is a training aid to help me improve. The same concept is what you will want to create with your avatar. Define the persona of what you believe the ideal conscious leader would be like and then match the ideal state to how you feel you are at for each characteristic today. This gap analysis will give you the areas you want to work on and build your action development plan to close the gap to your ideal state. To build your avatar start by visualizing your ideal transformational leader and answer these questions:

- What characteristics do they have that you appreciate?

- What special skills do they have?

- How do they behave?

- How do they speak and move?

- How do they respond and interact with others?

- When stuck or doing a certain activity, what would they do?

Take action with using your avatar as a coach. In the audio program Neurunner, from www.neurunner.com, they use NLP and other performance strategies to improve your confidence and running performance. One exercise was imagining having a discussion with someone whose advice you respect, asking them questions and picturing them responding. This is what you can do with your avatar. Use your avatar as your virtual training partner to support your growth in becoming the transformational leader you want to be.

Step eight: Take action. Transformational leaders take action. This entire book is filled with actions to take to support your own transformation and that of others. It begins with you taking action. Create a list of the top 10 actions you will take from your reading and pick one of them and do something immediately to create movement toward achieving the action. The things you do today, the books you read, the initiatives and projects you undertake and the people you spend time with is who you will be in three to five years and those will be your strengths. The actions you start today are critical to set yourself up for the success you want to have. A coach, mentor, accountability buddy or peer who has the ability to advise you on where you want to go is a great action you can take. Pick someone who has done what you want to do and you have rapport with. The value is they will challenge you to get beyond yourself to stick with your goals to be a transformational leader.

Transforming your team and organization

So far we have discussed your actions to becoming a transformational leader and the steps and things you can do to achieve it. Steve Jobs' quote "The journey is the reward" accents the actions you take will be rewarding as you expand your skills and knowledge. When you see the people you are helping shift and make positive changes in their lives, the feeling you have made a real difference is a true gift to receive. This section covers the actions you will take to transform your team and organization. The work you have done to shift yourself is the foundation to move an entire group. The personal attributes such as leading by example, being congruent, truly listening for understanding and being compassionate are critical to build the trust for others to follow your lead. If you are not inspired, others will not be inspired. You make the difference for an organization to shift with how you show up and what you do or don't do. The following four action areas are things that make a difference in transforming your teams to make a shift to perform and interact in a way that makes a positive difference for each member and for the greater good of your stakeholders who depend on the team.

Build esprit de corps. Morale of the group is an essential force of connecting people to a common bond and will last even in times of hardship or difficulty. If you have ever been part of a team that had a strong esprit de corps, the energy, the feeling of being connected and the willingness to do anything for each other is a moving experience. I have had this opportunity in the military, corporate environment and sports teams. The commonality between these organizations was having a shared mission we all needed to cooperate together to be successful. You could not be successful without the team pulling together to accomplish the mission. They also had an element of difficulty be it working on critical customers' network outage with stress levels being high, being under fire where your lives were on the line or how do we win the game to make it to the playoffs? When you have a strong sense of morale, even as new people join they will rise to the standards of the others in the team, because they can feel it and the group will demand it. It also becomes a team culture and is infectious. Building and maintaining morale is critical. It is easy to lose if the action such as layoffs, lost benefits and anything deemed as unjust happens. These erode trust and will negatively impact the morale, unless the leader is open and transparent about the reason for the changes throughout the entire transition. You build morale by focusing on the people first, having a common shared mission, building trust by fostering open communication, bringing the discussions people are having behind the scenes out into the open by having people share their views and get it all out, doing events together, sharing information about who they really are and many others. Your action is to assess where your team's morale is today and understand why. Then determine what actions can you take together to build more trust and interactions to get the team working together. For example, if you work in a virtual environment and the team members' work is individual focused today, create joint projects that get them to interact, collaborate and work as a team to achieve the goal. Having high esprit de corps where everyone cares for each other makes for a great working environment and creates better solutions for your clients.

Demonstrate what you want. To move a team or anyone you must show them where you want them to go. Clarity of what success looks like is essential for people to know how they can contribute to achieve it. Starting movement and trying to figure it out en route creates frustration and wastes resources. This also impacts morale and trust that the leader or greater organization knows what they are doing. This leads to people disengaging and doing what they are told. To create a fully engaged team that makes things happen there are actions the transformational leader can take to bring clarity to all the members.

- *Build a shared vision statement.* With your team build a vision of where you want to be in three to five years. This provides who, what, where and when of how the future will be. This is built to inspire and give the team the direction of what you want. This becomes the guiding light for the organization.

- *Communicate your intent.* Your intent is a description of the end-state that you want to achieve. Combining the vision statement and your intent is powerful to ensure clarity and that everyone knows what success looks like. An example can be at 17:00 hours today our flag is on top of that hill. This is very clear intent.

- *Use social media to reinforce the direction.* Reinforcing the message is important to keep the focus on what you are trying to accomplish. Written or video blogs, Twitter, post, discussion forums are all ways to get the message out and share examples of how it is being done across the industry or your company. People tend to need to hear things many times to process it and make it their own. Repeat your message to make it stick.

- **Role model success.** Being the example of the change you want others to be is critical. Your actions are very visible and if you are demonstrating the behaviors or actions you want the team to follow, they will take your lead and see it is important, because you are doing it.

- **Show what success looks like continuously.** The quickest way to get the behavior you want is to focus on it and reward it. Communicating the examples of the change you want and publically rewarding will help drive the results you want.

Plan and execute. What you plan, schedule, execute and inspect gets accomplished. Just as you plan the work initiatives and projects your team will implement for your stakeholders, planning the implementation of the transformation of your organization is valuable to making it happen. Taking action of assigning your top talent to the transformation you want to achieve sends a clear message of how important it is. How you spend your time and ensuring this area is part of your weekly schedule makes this a priority and demonstrates this to your organization. You will tend to get what you inspect and not what you expect. You have to show it is important by inspecting the results. What you focus on becomes infectious and this drives behavior. A way to begin is to review your vision and end state intent to determine what you want to be famous for. Some examples you may come up with include being transparent, open communication, risk taking, trust, teamwork etc. For each of these define what this means to you, what success looks like, what actions you are going to implement to achieve them and how you can tell you are on track. Actions you can take:

- During your all-hands meeting use one of the things you want to be famous for as the theme of the event and have speakers, stories and examples of what it means and who is being an example of demonstrating it.

- Create tiger teams of employees to come together and define actions that can be taken to implement and make changes to achieve the change you want to accomplish.

- Regularly post, blog, use discussion forums and other social media to keep the focus and demonstrate it is important and a priority.

- Make it part of your people's performance review that they will be responsible for their part of it to be a success.

- Survey your team on a regular basis so you can learn if you are on track. Share the results and follow-on actions with your team.

Become a feedback expert. Three main elements to achieving the performance you want to have are: ensuring the expectations are clearly set and acknowledged by the person; there is a consequence in place to drive what you want; and there is timely feedback on how they are doing. If any one of these is missing then there is a high likelihood you will not be getting the results you want. Mastering giving feedback is a skill that is a must to transform your organization. Without it you cannot achieve change. All of the personal characteristics of being a transformational leader are in play with being able to give feedback and have the person you are giving feedback to respect the message and you as the deliverer. If you have trust and respect then you can provide feedback that will move and shift people. Encouraging the team to give open feedback to each other is the factor that will transform teams. This means the team has the trust in each other and they do not make a personal assault on any one team member.

A very effective exercise that Gershon Mader, the president of Quantum Performance Inc., uses is bringing the background discussions to the foreground to build trust in organizations. In teams or as individuals a list of background discussions will be collected and in a group environment the list will be presented by saying the background discussion about the team or person for example, your team thinks only ideas they create are good ones or you mentioned you are open to feedback and you get defensive anytime someone disagrees with you. The person or team who is receiving the feedback will simply respond with thank you. The big idea is people live in these discussions every day and by making them visible the entire team can move beyond them. Having participated in this exercise I have found it refreshing and most of the issues were just caused by a misunderstanding that could be cleared up quickly. Having open feedback builds trust and this moves organizations to greater levels of cooperation and teamwork.

The benefit of transforming your team and organization is to create an environment where consciousness is the way of operating. This leads to an amazing working environment that inspires people to be their best every day. Water cooler chat conversations transform into deep and meaningful dialog that builds strong connections, increases people's energy and creates a new way of working for all the team members. Energy is freed from removing limiting team beliefs, distrust and petty rivalries, and is now transformed into driving innovation and change. A new paradigm of collaboration between the team members is created and this leads to making a positive difference for them and their stakeholders. Implementing the ideas we covered in this section will build a team that is flying in one formation and delivers amazing results.

Key Points

Your takeaway from this chapter is the actions and steps to guide you to becoming a transformational leader. We covered together:

- In being a transformational leader having the courage and making the inner choice to pursue your dreams and helping others to achieve theirs is vital to being successful.

- Mastery of your skills is the goal to be the best you can be. This includes the top 10 competencies and the core foundational psychographics that are a must to be able to connect with people and for them to follow your lead.

- To achieve mastery, building a development plan using the three horizons model brings simplicity and focus to the short-term, mid-term and long-term skills you desire to enhance.

- Using exposure, education and experience, along with using your strengths and things you enjoy, provides you an approach to define the activities that will make up your development plan.

- Building a transformational leader's playbook provides a reference and collection of material you want to practice and create positive enabling habits to support you.

- Tools such as planning, self-reflection, mindset, NLP basics to understand people better and the use of questions adds more items to the transformational leader's toolkit to drive change within the organization.

- The eight steps to facilitate becoming a transformational leader: set yourself up to win; role models; build your conscious network; know your special abilities; collaborate; take risk; virtual avatar; and take action.

- To transform your team and organization to fly in one formation together focus on building esprit de corps, demonstrate what you want, plan and execute and become a feedback expert.

CHAPTER 8

Organization Guidelines: Building A Conscious way

Conscious leading is a business must

A lot of companies and leaders mention that talent is an essential component for their success. There are a number of predictions of future shortages of talent, more competition to attract talent, and retaining talent is one of their top priorities. Yet the organizational processes, policies and old school methods of leadership still rule and run counter to what is needed to transform to a way of being a complete conscious organization. A conscious organization is one that is ethical in its business processes, a social citizen thinking of the wellbeing of all stakeholders, a leading example in the communities they operate, environmental focused in being good stewards of the natural resources they use and impact, giving back to others and growing their leaders and employees to live a well-balanced, healthy and productive life. The leaders of conscious organizations live by being examples of the components and attributes covered in this book. These leaders take their role of building a conscious organization very seriously and by doing so build a legacy of true greatness. They make conscious leading a must for their companies.

The three main areas that an organization can focus on to begin their journey toward becoming a conscious organization is their management selection and development, policies they implement and enforce and their culture. These three are interconnected. An example of this can be seen in Marco Nink's April 23, 2013 blog post in the Gallup Business Journal titled "Germany Has a Serious Management Problem," where Gallup's research shows that only 15% of German workers feel they are engaged at work. Employees feeling they are not engaged account for 61% and the remaining

24% are actively disengaged. Gallup estimates the 24% actively disengaged cost the German economy "112 billion to 138 billion euros per year in lost productivity." A key factor highlighted is the manager and the importance of the role they play in creating engaged employees. A practice by formal or informal policy in Germany is the person with the most seniority or the subject matter expert becomes the manager. The people selected to manage may have no aptitude to manage people, or as we have covered in this book no leader's mindset or even desire to lead people. The benefit to making a conscious way a must is increased employee engagement and greatly reducing the cost of absenteeism. In Marco Nink's April 26, 2013 blog post in the Gallup Business Journal titled "Low Employee Well-being and Engagement Hurt Germany Companies," employees who are engaged have nearly three times lower absenteeism compared to those who are actively disengaged. In that article, according to Frankfurter Allgemeine Zeitung, each day a person in Germany is absent from work it costs 275.20 euros a day to the business. The actively disengaged employee misses on average 10.7 days a year at a cost of 2,945 euros per employee a year. The employee who is engaged is absent on average 3.9 days a year with a cost of 1,073 euros. The cost savings benefit to the business is 64%.

Another area of cost savings can be found in replacement cost when someone leaves. Figures can be estimated at anywhere from 150% to 250% of the person's annual compensation. Here policies that are counterintuitive to truly taking care of people in a conscious way have an impact. Glen who is a senior director for a high-tech company explained to me how his best employee was being paid 25% below the mid-point for their grade, and after raising the matter many times with his leadership and human resources organization the answer he received back was giving such a pay increase was out of policy. The employee feeling underappreciated left to a competitor, where they received the amount they were looking for. Not including the lost knowledge and experience this cost, the losing company now has to find, hire and train the replacement at a much more significant cost than the 25% pay increase would have cost the company.

In another example in their fiscal Q1 starting in August 2013, a major high-tech company announced a 4,000-person workforce reduction. In 2014 the same company had a similar reduction. The interesting point was the move for both years was not intended as a cost saving move and the expectation was the company would actually have flat to slightly increased expenses over the next fiscal year. The main callout was the company felt they did not have the right people in the right places and as their internal processes to move people to other roles was ineffective, felt training the impacted people would not achieve the intent and moving people throughout the company is not embraced in the leadership culture. The company felt the best move was to let experienced people leave, and if they had the skills for the new areas, to be rehired as needed by those growth areas needing new people. Waiving the six-month waiting period in the U.S. to be rehired back reinforced this approach senior leadership chose. The cost of this decision included the exit packages and the cost of hiring new people for the new roles. The cost that will not be calculated is the impact of the people who were not let go and now feel disenfranchised and have become disengaged employees after some had seen up to 50% of their team impacted by the workforce reduction.

An old-school policy that feeds employee disengagement and lack of open communication that moves people to being their best is the practice that Jack Welch implemented when he was the CEO for General Electric Company of annually managing out the bottom 10% of the employees who are not living up to the expectations of their position. My 14 years' experience leading in a company system that focused on letting go of the bottom 5% annually is this practice generated policies to make up for the lack of selecting the right people managers and training managers on how to manage performance. When the culture or processes are not achieving what senior leadership expects, the lever most often used is to create policy to force the change. When this occurs you do not get what you expected. What this policy creates is untrained managers who know they have to come up with a bottom 5% each year and this leads them to identify who the candidates are to fill this requirement, and rather than work with them more to raise the employees' performance, they do the opposite and tend to separate themselves from the identified group. The separation was to make it easier to be emotionally disconnected to let the person go later. However, the impact on the person in the zone of being in the bottom 5% is confusion, lack of communication and normally surprise and disbelief when they are informed they are in the bottom 5%. I have had employees join my team who were identified as being non-performers and it would never fail that when I spoke to these people no one ever communicated anything to them. Once they had the feedback the change was always amazing to watch. The added problem these types of policies create is when you compound this by every team in the company who is doing this, you constantly have a group of disengaged employees and lost productivity that adds cost to the company.

The examples above show how cost, employee disengagement, losing good people and lost productivity are just a few of the reasons that conscious leading and transforming your organization is a business must. Leaders set the example and your transformation is the essential ingredient to become the beacon for your people and organization to follow. As a leader you get what you inspect and not always what you expect until it becomes a living component of your culture. Your inspection process begins by selecting the right people managers, ensuring you have the development program and plans in place to get the best out of your people, and having policies that enable a conscious way are all essential components to having the highly engaged workers you want to succeed as a business. This chapter will give you ideas on how you can build a conscious leading way in your organization.

Conscious leadership leading indicators

The concept, terminology and use of conscious leadership in the corporate environment are in the early stages of awareness. When I discuss conscious leadership concepts with other leaders I find I have to spend time defining what it means and how it applies to their business. It is not yet common language within organizations today. Terms such as emotional intelligence, corporate responsibility and inclusion, and diversity are already commonly used language and are fairly well understood. Most of these already have programs established and leaders who are responsible for their implementation and management. I believe conscious leadership is the future trend that we will see as the programs of the near future and a major focus of businesses to help drive their success. Leading indicators such as government policy, mainstream books, movements and educational programs are gearing up for this new mindset way of being and leading. These all provide sources of information for building your organization's program and becoming a thought leader in this growing domain.

We are already seeing the focus on consciousness in government policy. The State of Delaware on August 1, 2013 implemented a new law, which John Montgomery's blog post on the same day titled "A Giant Step Forward for Sustainability and Human Consciousness" (www.greatfromthestart. com), highlights that "authorizes the formation of corporations endowed with a comprehensive corporate conscience that protects the interest of society and the environment in addition to those of stockholders." John further states "the new law imposes a tri-partite balancing requirement on directors to balance: (i) the traditional pecuniary interests of stockholders; (ii) the interests of those affected by corporate behavior; and (iii) the one or more public benefits adopted by the corporation in its charter. Directors of public benefit corporations have an additional fiduciary duty to their stockholders to balance these three purposes." This leading indicator demonstrates that being conscious and focusing on the greater good of others besides the stockholders is going to be mandatory and not an option in the future.

The subject of consciousness is being seen more and more in books and the movements they are generating. In the book *Conscious Capitalism* by John Mackey and Raj Sisodia they demonstrate how great companies such as Whole Foods Market, Google, Southwest Airlines, Costco, UPS and others are being successful by focusing on creating value for all their stakeholders by using the four elements of having a higher purpose, stakeholder integration, conscious leadership, and conscious culture and management. Not only has the book been very successful, it has also generated a movement where you can participate in local chapters in the U.S. or internationally to discuss, share information and collaborate on consciousness. More information can be found on their website (www. consciouscapitalism.org/community). Another example is the book and movie titled *Choice Point* by Harry Massey and David R. Hamilton PhD. Their work on aligning your purpose and making a choice to create a positive change in the world has also created a social media movement where people come together to share and collaborate on solutions (www. choicepointmovement.com). Both of these leading indicators show the excitement that is being generated around finding your purpose, being conscious and taking action by participating in the social movements that have resulted from people being inspired to want to learn and do more.

Education provides another leading indicator of how the focus on consciousness is becoming part of the curriculum to teach leaders of the future the importance of both achieving your professional goals while being conscious and making a change to build a better world. Dr. Marko Saravanja was a monk who practiced the traditions of the Ananda Marga yoga and meditation, and moved to South Africa in 1991 from Croatia. The idea he had was to create a conscious university that not only focused on developing one's intellect but also included developing the emotional, physical and spiritual self. In 1998 Regenesys Business School (http://regenesys.co.za) was created. Over the last 16 years they have educated more than 85,000 students with their approach that also is intended to inspire the students' hearts and souls. They emphasize developing positive values, attitudes and behaviors as part of their educational program. This is highlighted on their home page: "A Regenesys graduate is an analytical thinker, problem-solver, emotionally intelligent and values-driven leader who is able to operate successfully in a dynamic global environment." The big idea is by making the elements of consciousness part of the learning process, these future leaders will already be equipped to lead their organization through the process of embracing conscious leading. These students who have had this integrated learning will also be great candidates to reverse mentor other leaders who have been in the company longer and have not been exposed to these concepts and approaches. An example of reverse mentoring is when my children were teenagers they would teach me how to use smart devices etc. The intent is to have the employees who have the knowledge and experience through their education to be part building and supporting your conscious leading program.

The above examples are a snapshot of the activity that is already occurring to make conscious leading part of our natural way of being. They are an indication of more to come and are intended to spark your ideas on what the future can bring now that you are well on your own journey to becoming a conscious leader. The next section is focused on what you can begin to do to build your organizational program to expand your growth and the growth of those around you.

Conscious leadership program components

To implement any successful program into a company, the change and adoption framework that you normally use also applies with deploying your consciousness program components. The areas of special attention that need to be applied are to ensure the program is a top priority and people are held accountable throughout the entire business for its success. A method that tends to work well here is to assign your top talent to leading the program. Nothing indicates the importance of a project or initiative better than when you assign your top people to lead its implementation. Other techniques are to make it part of people's annual evaluation, a prominent subject in every business review and all-hands presentation, and having active social forums and support groups that are facilitated to encourage sharing information and best practices. When all the employees are using the language of consciousness on a regular basis, this is a good indicator your program is on a successful track.

The other areas of special focus are to have senior leadership's continuous support and be seen leading the priority; have clear expectations established and communicated on who is doing what and by when; have measureable and tangible outcomes; and establish the recognition, rewards and policies to enable the success. All of these need to be part of your business plan for implementing your program. The main three components of your conscious program that I will cover in this section include:

- **New Hire Phase** – practices to identify the employees and leaders who best represent who you want as part of your team.

- **Development Phase** – ideas on how to encourage, provide support and develop people to use and master the leadership competencies.

- **Sustainment Phase** – thoughts on keeping your program's momentum moving in the direction you want it.

To build a program the first step is to know what you really want to achieve. This vision or mission statement will become your guide to identifying what components you will want to implement and by when. Two tools that can help here are conducting a SWOT analysis of the current situation and a visioning exercise of what the future looks like when you have succeeded. The purpose of the SWOT analysis is to give you an assessment of your current situation by capturing the internal to your organization elements (Strengths and Weaknesses) and the external environment's components (Opportunities and Threats). To guide you with using this tool here is a brief explanation and example of each component of the SWOT analysis tool:

- **Strengths:** these are characteristics that you believe give you an advantage. This could include a strong company culture and values that people live every day, open communication where people freely express their opinions for the better of the team, high emotional intelligence etc.

- **Weaknesses:** any characteristics that place the team at a disadvantage. This could include a lack of trust among employees and leadership, hierarchal culture, feedback only during formal reviews etc.

- **Opportunities:** things that can be used to create an advantage. By implementing this program what value can this give us as a team? This could be creating new relationships with your stakeholders using the same attributes of open and enriched feedback, finding new ways of incorporating your customers' feedback into your development program, extending your program to include customers and partners, and other elements.

- **Threats:** these are things that can negatively impact your company or cause issues to your business. Another way to look at this is what if we don't implement this program? As highlighted earlier, the new law implemented in Delaware can be a threat if you are legally required to change your business practices.

With your SWOT assessment you will have a good view of what you can build on within your team and what you need to include as part of your program. With this current view, the visioning exercise helps you to identify what success looks like in the future. In Chapter 6 under the new way of leading others, I introduced the exercise call Future Pace, which you can use to imagine what the future will look like after implementing your program. The intent is to define your success and then to backwards plan from that time to highlight the milestones you will need to achieve along the way. For example, if you believe it will take three years to implement your program, when you backwards plan from then to today's current moment, what needs to be completed in year one and by each quarter and in year two and three by each quarter to achieve your plan. This exercise not only gives you your vision of the future, but also helps build the framework of your implementation plan by each quarter and year. Once you have an idea of what you want to achieve you can choose the elements from the three phases you want to include in your plan.

The New Hire Phase. As we covered in Chapter 5, everyone is a leader. In this phase the key ideas are on selecting the right people to join your organization. You have used the Future Pace exercise to identify what success will look like; an important aspect is who are the people in your vision that are making it come true? In Chapter 7, step seven to becoming a transformational leader is to build your own virtual avatar or persona. Expanding on this exercise is an idea for creating the personas that are important for your team. You can have as many as you need. For sure one would need to be for your leadership positions. In building the persona what characteristics are important? What special skills do they need to have? How do they behave? How do they need to be? How do they respond and interact with others? And any other attributes or aspects that you feel are critical. The persona becomes your guide for hiring new people into your organization and becomes the mentor for others who are already in the team to aspire to. Thus it helps you in the next phase of building your development programs. If you find creating the persona is challenging, you can use the Neuro-Linguistic Programing (NLP) technique of modeling to help. Basically modeling is observing people who are really good at what they do and determining what makes them successful. The point is if you ask people they normally cannot tell you exactly what it is they do that makes them good at it. By observing you can find the traits and things they do and build this into your persona. In his book titled *Managing with the Power of NLP*, David Molden explains how the company Computacenter successfully modeled their IT service engineers to find out whom and what traits did they display that delivered the best customer satisfaction. They then used this as a hiring criterion and saw an overall increase in their customer satisfaction scores by matching the right people to the role based on what was already successful from their modeling. Thus if you already have someone who best represents the persona you want to create, modeling them can be a great starting point.

Assuming the people you hire can actually do the work you need them to do, the big three for ensuring you find the right members are trust, values match and being open. Is the person's foundation built on trusting others and being able to foster trust? Without trust the type of openness and feedback that moves people, as we have discussed in the book, will not be achieved. In one position, I had a group of employees join a new team we were building. When I discussed with them what was the key element they wanted to have in our team and did not think they had with their last leader, every single one said trust. This held them back as a team and they were not able to commit fully because they looked at their leader's actions with suspicion. The second must is the person has to match and live the values you want to represent. Value mismatch is the most critical reason why people do not succeed and are unable to be their best. My personal experience for changing organizations has always been a result of a values mismatch. My values at one time were aligned, yet the organization's values can change as the business gets bigger and leaders are selected or hired that do not represent the core values that founded the company, and changes begin to occur. The third big element is openness in sharing with others and being open with their communications. Without open communication, achieving a conscious way with all your stakeholders will not happen. If people feel you are holding information back and you are unwilling to have the hard discussions about what is happening, this will create an environment lacking trust and others will hold back also. How do you find if a candidate matches these big three criteria and others that you find are important? The best way is through assessment.

Using your modeling of traits that you identified using the technique above, the big three and other attributes essential for your candidate, first identify all the must criteria the person must have. A must criteria means if they do not fit a must they are immediately disqualified. This could be values mismatch, teamwork, trust or others. Define what is meant by each must item with a description and examples so all those involved in the hiring process are clear what they mean. Next identify your wants. What attributes would you want from the candidate and again define these. The difference is a want is not necessarily a disqualification and can be a development area such as knowing a specific software package etc. With your criteria defined determine the level of investment to identify the method of assessment for the candidates. The simplest and yet not the most effective is to conduct behavior-based interviews where your interviewers have the person demonstrate with their answers they can do the behavior you are looking for. The others are either using a test, assessment center day or hiring a third party to simulate and go deeper into how the person really works and behaves. As leaders selection is so essential for your program I advocate having a third party such as the company Corporate Psychologists (www.corporatepsychologists.com) be involved in determining if the leader will be able to achieve what you need before hiring them. They can help create 360-degree assessment exercises that actually test how the candidates will react under stress in the work environment and provide another data point on the person you are looking to hire. The investment is worth having the right leaders to ensure your employees are in the fully engaged category and performing their best. When your people are at their best the company thrives.

The Development Phase. This phase is about building an ongoing program to train the conscious skills and ensure they become part of how people are on a daily basis. Your assessment of the strengths and weaknesses of where you are today is a good starting point to determine your overall needs. For this phase I will recommend things that can make up your program focused on the individual, leaders and team.

Focusing on the individual's development is the foundation for all your employees to build skills, be exposed to new experiences and remove the barriers that are holding them back from achieving their personal greatness. It is best to make this a two-way effort to where the employee is responsible for his or her own development and as an organization you provide the access to resources to help them achieve their development goals. The following are four components to include in your program:

- **Personal Change Experience.** The idea is to provide an experience where your team members can be exposed to an opportunity where they realize they have a personal choice of continually living in the past or making a change to embrace something different. This choice has significant personal benefits to the person and builds flexibility to change, which is an essential business need. Dr. Joe Dispenza, whose books, seminars and programs are focused on personal transformation and use of meditation has created a program called "Breaking the Habit of Being Yourself," which is a one-day workshop delivered by certified trainers to provide this experience of a change transformation. When the individual sees change as a possibility and has a moving personal experience, this is where the magic begins to happen and change flexibility is developed. This type of program is a great way to begin building a change mentality in your business.

- **Co-Active Coaching.** Coaching is essential to mastering skills and being at the top of your game in whatever you do. For becoming fulfilled, finding your inner happiness and getting the most from life I have found the co-active coaching model and certified coaches to be a major help. On the Coaches Training Institute's (CTI) website they best explain the model when they state, "The Co-Active Model balances self-awareness, a keen agility with relationships, and courageous action to create an environment where individuals can be deeply fulfilled, connected to others and successful in what matters most." The intent is by providing this type of coaching to your people you are helping them to unlock their full potential, minimize their limiting beliefs and be happier, which results in them being better in all aspects of their lives and helps them bring their best every day to work.

- **Emotional Release Coaching.** We discussed earlier in this book the value of letting go of the emotions of events in your past using techniques like Emotional Freedom Techniques (EFT) and Matrix Reimprinting. We used an example of a sales person who goes to each sales call with the baggage of every other call they have ever made, and by releasing any subconscious routines or emotions those past calls have created, they enter the new sales call being at their best. Providing this type of coaching resource allows your team members to work on releasing the beliefs and emotions that are holding them back. As they release these limiting beliefs their confidence soars and so does their performance in their work.

- **Conscious Academy.** The concept is to build a curriculum of the skills you want as part of your program and persona you created earlier and provide a program to help your people acquire the knowledge. You are looking to build a roadmap of skills for each role you have in your organization and what is the best way to achieve it. A way to start is to pick the top 10 competencies you want to focus on and define what each one is and give examples of how you would see this being displayed in the work environment. For each competency, sub-define what a master, intermediate or beginner who is able to demonstrate that classification for each element would look like. For each of these sub-categories what trainings, experience or exposure activities can the person perform to achieve that level? This framework becomes your training program and clearly shows your people what it takes and what is available to master each competency.

Leaders need the same elements discussed in the individual components and also require an understanding of how those elements contribute to developing the individual and team. Thus your program must include leader training in how to implement your program, the business benefits, assessing employees' development needs and providing feedback that moves people. The two additional elements are giving the leaders the ability to role play the skills, which I'll cover more in the team aspects of the program, and having a continual 360-degree review process that becomes an essential ingredient to the leader's development plan. Providing executive coaching to make the 360-degree feedback an actionable development plan is recommended, as most self-managed 360-degree feedback programs companies use today do not deliver real change. This is because the person who is determining their own development plan from the feedback either has never seen a great example to mirror or does not know how to approach it. Providing a skilled coach to assist your leaders will help build development plans that will get better results for the person and organization.

The best way I have seen to develop teams is to put them in the environment that simulates what they could expect and to test different contingencies and worst-case scenarios. The U.S. military does this very well at their National Training Centers where they have professional opposing forces and actors who role play conditions you can expect in different combat situations. As a leader going through one of these exercises, you and your team play as though it is real and the learning is tremendous. If you have a crack in your team these experiences will find it quickly and make it a crater. This is what makes them so powerful, because you will learn what needs to be changed and each team member gains the experience to be able to change. You can build scenarios or hire companies who can do these role-plays with you. For example, to test their ability to handle a crisis management situation Volvo Construction Equipment (VCE) used Kreab & Gavin Anderson Worldwide to design a training exercise to test their management's ability to handle an extraordinary emergency situation. The exercise focused on leadership, communication and human reactions and was seen as a valuable learning experience by the people who participated. A simulation is the closest to real life situations that you can use to provide leaders and teams a safe environment to play and practice techniques they can then use every day on the job.

The Sustainment Phase. This phase of your program covers the activities that continue to make your program a focus and ongoing success. We have covered a few areas already such as ensuring you have success measurements, making it part of people's performance evaluation, part of business reviews and prominently mentioned in your employee all-hands meetings. We have all seen a number of initiatives that launch well with the ticket tape parade and as soon as leadership stops discussing it or focusing on it the initiative struggles. Thus continuous leadership focus and communication is critical. A new element that can bring real focus on having great leadership is to implement a managers' rating system by their employees that is visible to the entire organization. By modifying your on-line directory employees can rate their leaders, like on Amazon using a five-star system and leaving comments. These are then visible to everyone and people looking to work for that leader can see what others have to say and how they were perceived. This puts responsibility for being a great leader a priority and makes it visible feedback to everyone. This can be expanded to including peer feedback on both leaders and individuals. The idea is building an open feedback culture and demonstrating its importance by making it visible to everyone.

These components along with successful elements you already have in place will allow you to launch a great program that will bring great value to your people and organization. Your flexibility to change will become your competitive advantage in the fast-paced world we are in today. You will become aware of the shifts that your program is generating when things that used to occupy your thoughts no longer do, and you hear the language of conscious change being discussed throughout the organization.

Building a sustainable conscious way

Be it for you, your team or organization, the first major step is to begin taking action and use the techniques and tools we have discussed in this book to get you on your way. By being in motion from taking action you will gain forward progress and as you start seeing the results true momentum will take over. This momentum becomes fuel for you staying the course. Not to sugarcoat it, sustaining your conscious way takes you being committed, having will power, discipline and following through with your actions. To not be overwhelmed and hoping to short cut from your start point to destination, which will not work, success is created by doing a few small actions daily. These small steps build on each other and start to create greater achievements. Before you know it you have generated major changes in your life. The true intent is as Eddie Cantor highlights: "Slow down and enjoy life. It's not only the scenery you miss by going too fast – you also miss the sense of where you are going and why." Take it slow and deliberate and you will sustain your journey and enjoy all the marvelous new things you will be learning about yourself, others and the world.

There are a number of techniques you can use to build a sustainable action plan to keep you, your team or organization on track to achieving your goals. I encourage you to add to the list below of things that work for you and please share your examples. This list represents things that I have found to work for me and other organizations.

Commit – Schedule in Advance. For my marathon training and running I find that by planning for the event, registering and paying the cost for the race, booking the flights and hotel, I have skin in the game. This commitment means I have a date in the calendar that I need to be ready by to run the race. As I want to make it an enjoyable moment and have a good or great time, I know I need to do the miles of training to be ready. When my alarm goes off at 05:00 and my inner voice tells me how more sleep will make me feel even better, my commitment and yes, thinking of the pain of the last third of the marathon by not being prepared, I get up. The act of just getting up starts my routine and soon I'm out the door running regardless of the weather. You can use this for many events or activities in your life, such as committing and scheduling to attend a seminar, class, coaching session, sporting event, trip, time with others and anything you want to achieve.

Adopt a just do it and don't think about it mentality. "Take your life in your own hands and what happens? A terrible thing: no one to blame." – Erica Jong. Sometimes the simplest thing is to just take charge of your life, do the task and not think about it. Motivation and dedication are habits that form when you are doing the task over and over, which is leading you to mastery. When I changed my training program to start running six days a week and added a sprint and a tempo run, my mind created a lot of chatter when I was running the hard sessions. What helped me through it was to just do the session as planned and not think about it. This worked to keep my inner critic quiet and as I started to see the impact that these sessions were having to my overall running, I was motivated to do more.

Do it with someone and get others involved. Success is created through the performance of a few small daily disciplines that stack up over time to provide achievements far beyond anything you could have ever planned for. The key is doing the work and if you are motivated by doing it with others, then join a team, club or invite a friend to do the activities with you. Make it a social event and include others. In the work environment this can be having brown bag lunch sessions together, best practices sharing sessions or buddy teams mentoring each other. Get as many people as possible involved in helping you achieve your goals and you helping them. The community approach will increase your energy just by being around people on a similar path that you are on and encouraging each other to be your best.

Be an example. Leadership by its nature means you are an example for others. The keys to sustaining success are maintaining your focus. What three things can you do every day that support building the success habits to maintain your, the team's and organization's growth? Two other important questions to ask yourself while you are setting the example each day is what can you measure that demonstrates you are getting what you want? Being aware is the first step to measuring. How can you be each day with your actions, communication and support of others to be an example? Your actions and how you show up each day means much more than what you say. Everything you do is an example one way or the other, good or bad. The choice is yours.

Reach for the top of the mountain. Dare to dream and live your dream each day. With your team or as an individual create your vision statement that will drive you toward your dream and identify the strategies you will use to get there. The execution to make it happen then is all the activities you will take to achieve the strategies you have created. This is your plan and along the route of your journey there will be checkpoints or benchmarks that you will define that will show you if you are on track or not. If not, change to get back on track. If you are doing better than you expected, what caused this so you can do even more of it. This approach brings your dreams to reality and allows you to achieve your goals. Dream big by reaching for the mountain and take action to make it happen.

Reward the behavior you want. You get what you inspect and what you reward. When you achieve a goal or milestone in your development take the time to reflect, celebrate the achievement and reward yourself for a job well done. This habit builds your confidence and motivation toward this success cycle. With your teams build in the rewards and celebration points to acknowledge the successes they are making and achieving along your organization's path to a conscious way. Truly appreciate others by letting them know what you are seeing in them and how they are being when they model the behaviors that are the foundation of your team's values. This helps to build the mindset and culture toward getting more of the same successful behaviors. You will get more of what is recognized and rewarded. I have seen in teams where the people who were receiving all the recognition were the ones doing project work which was not the team's core responsibility. Once people saw this, everyone wanted to be on projects. Building this into your plan upfront will help to sustain your success.

Managing transition is a key to change. In his book *Managing Transitions: Making the Most of Change,* William Bridges explains how successful changes occur within the business when people are clear on the purpose, they have a plan for the change and are actively involved. The leader plays an essential role in helping people see how their job changes and how the change benefits them and their stakeholders. A number of change efforts fail to take into account the impact the change will have on the person and the loss they can experience from the new way of doing business. In one example I was involved with, the organization was changing from a support by email case handling method to using an automated case handling system. The benefits for tracking and visibility were very clear to all stakeholders. The challenge on why it took two years to get traction with the change was no one took into account the people who were to use and make the new system successful felt they lost their identity from their clients knowing them from their personal email support to being hidden behind a tool. Once the implementation team became aware they were able to work with each person on their transition and the program became a big success. The key takeaway is leaders taking into account the psychological aspects of a change on the people involved is a key skill to develop.

Smart policies. The policies you implement can destroy any program or momentum you are creating or become an enabling force to drive greater successes. Careful construction is key to any policies you plan to implement. A policy can live a long time after its purpose of why it was created has long passed. In an earlier example, the manager who could not get his star employee who was under the mid-point and below the other team members a pay raise, due to company policy, left for a competitor. The cost of finding, hiring, training and integrating a replacement person far outweighed making up the difference and paying the employee the mid-point. To counter this, the first step is to ask is the policy worth the juice of implementing it or are we adding policy to make up for the lack of training? For example, if your policy requires employees to wash their cars on a regular basis to be ready in case they have a customer visit and no one will inspect or hold them accountable to do it, ask if this is worth it to create the policy. The second step is to look at the policy does it reward the right behavior, punish the right behavior, or has no impact on the behavior you want. Contingency test the policy to see if it gives you what you really want and plan to recheck it after a predefined period to see if it is still effective or not. The third step is to ensure the feedback loop is built in and effective. Having policy with no feedback to the people who are to use it leads to ineffective policy. As policies can have such an impact on the success of your program and your culture, smart plan policies that are only absolutely required into your program and drop the rest.

Use technology to enable your program. Technology can enable your program and assist in driving the adoption. This can be in forms of interactive community forums, providing website information, sharing ideas and allowing others to contribute and endorse the ideas of others. Technology allows more people, regardless of where they are to participate, to be active and benefit from your program's different building blocks. Enabling your leaders by having them use video blogs, video messaging, Twitter-type updates and other tools all helps to demonstrate the importance of what you are trying to achieve and sets the example for the organization.

This list represents a few of the many creative ideas you and your team can come up with to build a program that will achieve the results you want for your people and all stakeholders. This chapter provided you the foundation to take conscious leadership from an individual journey and being a leader that makes a difference for all stakeholders and society, to building your plan to have your entire business operating in a new way of being. This new way of being is whatever you dare to dream. Get creative, get with others and imagine what your conscious organization will look like, how people will interact with each other, what people will be saying and doing, and how you will be making a difference in the world. My dream is that this book will enable you to embrace, adopt, create and live the life that you choose that makes you happy and fulfilled. **You are Conscious Leadership In Action!**

Key Points

Your takeaway from this chapter is conscious leadership is a business must and by using the guiding components you can build a successful program for your organization. We covered together:

- Conscious leading is essential to be competitive to attract talent, keep your talent engaged, be cost effective, and become a great example of a business that acts in the best interest for all of societies' stakeholders.

- Three main areas an organization can focus on to become a conscious company is with their management selection and how they develop their leaders, the policies they implement and hold people accountable for, and their culture.

- Delaware's government policy focused on requiring companies to be more conscious and new innovative ways to incorporate consciousness into the education program being offered to students with the example of the Regenesys Business School in South Africa are some of the leading indicators of the change we are experiencing toward being more conscious.

- By using tools such as the SWOT (Strengths, Weaknesses, Opportunities and Threats) analysis, you can assess your current business situation to determine where you can begin to build your conscious program for your company.

- Along with your leaders being fully engaged and setting the example, three phases with suggested components can be used to formulate your implementation plan. The three phases are: New Hire Phase, Development Phase, and Sustainment Phase.

- Building a sustainable conscious way provided many techniques you can use and add to ensure your program gains traction and maintains momentum once implemented.

Conclusion

Congratulations on completing this book! If you have completed the exercises and work throughout this journey you and I have taken together, you have a really great awareness about yourself and what works best for you. You will have a number of actions, rituals and a plan you can use each day to give you the energy to fuel your life transformation. You can have the life of your dreams. All you have to do it dare to dream it, claim it, as it is yours to live and make it a reality by taking action. Everyone can do this; it just needs you to take the first step. You deserve to have the life you want. Be the best you can be and have fun with it!

What's next for you? As you embrace a conscious life focus, if your experiences are anything like mine, I have found that my life purpose and journey continue to provide me with new learnings every day. Being curious and looking at the world from a child's heart allows me to get to know more and more wonderful people and incredible things to experience. Focusing on consciousness and being in the moment brings more happiness, way less stress and a real fulfillment. Spending time with people who are on their own path gives me even more energy. Seeing the leading indicators that people and organizations are choosing to be more conscious and the movements that are being generated by people like you and me are all encouraging signs of greater things to come our way. I wish you the best on your journey to having the life of your dreams that is just right for you and gives you the peace you want.

All the best being a **Conscious Leader In Action!**

About The Author

Floyd W. Carlson began his conscious leadership journey when on the battlefields in Iraq. In an instant, his life changed forever. He saw his life flash before his eyes during the heat of a battle. When he thought his life was over, the vision that stood out the most was seeing an image of his son who had not been born yet. This game-changing event became his story that is driving his personal transformation. Floyd shares the experiences he has had and the things he has learned in this book **Conscious Leadership In Action!**

Floyd is presently a business executive serving as Director of Learning and Organizational Development for manufacturing company, Greenheck. Prior to this position he spent 15 years in Belgium working for Cisco Systems in various operations leadership roles for Cisco's Europe, Middle East, Africa and Russia organization. He led a number of cross-cultural teams in Cisco focused on solving customers' most important business problems.

Floyd has been leading teams for over 27 years. Prior to Cisco, he served 13 years in the U.S. army and was an airborne, ranger, infantry officer, who served in Germany, Operation Desert Storm, Panama and commanded two companies in the 101st Screaming Eagles Airborne Division.

Floyd's passion is spending time with his family, coaching and running. To date he has run 15 marathons.

CPSIA information can be obtained at www.ICGtesting.com
Printed in the USA
LVOW10s2118080615

441649LV00001B/1/P